CULTURES OF THE WORLD

Belize

Leslie Jermyn and Yong Jui Lin

Marshall Cavendish
Benchmark
New York

PICTURE CREDITS
Cover: © Bill Bachmann / Alamy
ANA: 39 • Audrius Tomonis: 138 • Corbis: 24, 31, 40, 41, 65, 71, 74, 106, 131 • Dave G. Houser: 98 • David Simson: 27, 32, 38, 43, 119 • Getty Images: 10, 18, 19, 25, 33, 35, 36, 44, 66, 86, 111 • Inmagine.com: 20, 54 • Jon Arnold Images Ltd / Photolibrary: 110 • Lonely Planet Images: 60, 99 • National Geographic Society Images: 17, 91 • North Wind Picture Archives: 21, 22, 23 • Photolibrary: 1, 3, 5, 6, 7, 8, 9, 11, 12, 13, 14, 15, 16, 26, 28, 29, 30, 37, 42, 45, 46, 47, 48, 49, 50, 51, 52, 53, 56, 57, 58, 59, 61, 62, 63, 64, 67, 68, 70, 72, 73, 75, 76, 77, 79, 80, 81, 82, 83, 84, 85, 87, 88, 89, 92, 93, 94, 95, 96, 97, 100, 101, 102, 103, 104, 105, 107, 108, 112, 113, 114, 115, 116, 117, 118, 120, 121, 122, 124, 125, 126, 127, 128, 129, 130

PRECEDING PAGE
Starfish bask in the crystal blue waters of Belize.

Publisher (U.S.): Michelle Bisson
Editors: Deborah Grahame-Smith, Peter Mavrikis, Mindy Pang
Copyreader: Daphne Hougham
Designers: Nancy Sabato, Benson Tan
Cover picture researcher: Tracey Engel
Picture researcher: Joshua Ang

Marshall Cavendish Benchmark
99 White Plains Road
Tarrytown, NY 10591
Website: www.marshallcavendish.us

© Times Media Private Limited 2001
© Marshall Cavendish International (Asia) Private Limited 2011
® "Cultures of the World" is a registered trademark of Times Publishing Limited.

Originated and designed by Times Media Private Limited
An imprint of Marshall Cavendish International (Asia) Private Limited
A member of Times Publishing Limited

Marshall Cavendish is a trademark of Times Publishing Limited.

All Internet sites were correct and accurate at the time of printing. All monetary figures in this publication are in U.S. dollars.

Library of Congress Cataloging-in-Publication Data
Jermyn, Leslie.
  Belize / Leslie Jermyn and Yong Jui Lin. — 2nd ed.
      p. cm. — (Cultures of the world)
  Includes bibliographical references and index.
  Summary: "Provides comprehensive information on the geography, history,
    wildlife, governmental structure, economy, cultural diversity, peoples,
    religion, and culture of Belize"—Provided by publisher.
  ISBN 978-1-60870-452-1
  1. Belize—Juvenile literature. I. Yong, Jui Lin. II. Title.
  F1443.2.J47 2012
  972.82—dc22   2010035966

Printed in China
7 6 5 4 3 2 1

CONTENTS

INTRODUCTION

BELIZE, OR BRITISH HONDURAS AS IT USED TO BE KNOWN, IS A fascinating country on the seaward eastern side of the Central American isthmus. It is unique in the region because, unlike its neighbors, it has a British cultural and linguistic tradition instead of a Spanish one. It is a tiny country, the most sparsely populated in Central America, but does not lack natural and social diversity. Its low population density is working well, as Belize's natural environment is very well preserved. Sadly, this pristine country is still not immune to the effects of global warming and climate change. Belize is a land of immigrants, past and present. People have come to live here to reap the bounties of nature and sometimes to escape difficult circumstances in their homelands. Today, Belize stands as an example of a culturally and ecologically diverse nation adapting to the modern world. In this book, we will explore how Belize became an English-speaking corner of Spanish Central America, learn about the current challenges and problems faced by this tiny state in the global economy, and come to admire some of its natural and cultural wonders.

GEOGRAPHY

Less than 10 feet (3 m) above sea level, Half Moon Cay in Belize is teeming with life. Home to colonies of seabirds, numbering in the thousands, this cay's southern beaches are also where the endangered loggerhead and hawksbill turtle lay their eggs.

BELIZE IS A POCKET-SIZE COUNTRY on the Caribbean side of the Central American isthmus, just south of the Yucatán Peninsula. The country has a coastline of about 240 miles (386 kilometers), and occupies an area of 8,867 square miles (22,966 square km), which is slightly smaller than Massachusetts.

An aerial view of a meandering river and heavy forest cover in Belize.

Besides the Maya Mountains, Belize's natural topography consists largely of limestone. The surrounding hilly limestone region around the Maya Mountains, for example, is characterized by numerous sinkholes, caverns, underground streams, and fertile soils—some of which have been cultivated for over 4,000 years.

Bordered on the north and northwest by Mexico, on the south and west by Guatemala, and on the east by the Caribbean Sea, it is the only Central American country with no access to the Pacific Ocean. The population of Belize is approximately 314,522, and its capital city is Belmopan. Although small, Belize has a diverse landscape and many beautiful geographical features, including the world's second largest barrier reef (199 miles or 320 km long) running parallel to the coast. The country also is the host of some rare species of plants and animals.

PHYSICAL ENVIRONMENT

There are three main physical regions in Belize: the northern lowlands, the southern highlands, and the coastal areas, including offshore islands and atolls. The northern half of the country, where the districts (the equivalent of states) of Corozal, Belize, and Orange Walk are located, is gently undulating, low-lying land. The main rivers there are the Hondo in the far north, and the New, Sibun, and Belize rivers. Most of Belize's agricultural production takes place in this region, and some deciduous forest remains intact.

Called "the most remarkable reef in the West Indies" by Charles Darwin in 1842, the Belize Barrier Reef is a series of coral reefs, stretching 199 miles (320 km) along the coast.

The southern half of the mainland of Belize is a highland plateau with the Maya Mountains running like a spine up the middle in a north-south direction. The Cockscomb Range is an outcropping of quartz and granite hills on the northeast of this plateau. Belize's highest point was said to be Victoria Peak, with a height of 3,851 feet (1,174 meters) in the Cockscomb range. A more recent survey, however, determined that Doyle's Delight, in the main cleft of the Maya Mountains, stands taller by 124 feet (38 m) at 3,805 feet (1,160 m). Most of the plateau is limestone overgrown by jungle, with many fast-running streams and rivers. The main rivers here are the Monkey, Deep, Grande, Moho, and Sarstoon.

The third region is the most settled, and includes the coastal mainland and the small islands and atolls offshore. The longest barrier reef in the Western Hemisphere is located 10 to 20 miles (16—32 km) offshore, beginning at Ambergris Caye in the north. Islands in Belize are called cays and make up approximately 212 square miles (549 square km) of the national territory, running the length of the country. Some lie inside the barrier reef, while others, such as the Turneffe Islands, are seaward of the reef. Given Belize's history as a trading port, most settlement has taken place along the coast and on the cays. Some cays are so small and low lying that they are nothing more than outcrops of coral, while others, such as Caulker and Ambergris cays, are larger, palm-covered tropical paradises.

Named after the peoples who fled there from the invading Spaniards, the Mayan Mountains are a range of hills that extend about 70 miles (113 km) from the Guatemalan border northwesward into central Belize.

CLIMATE AND SEASONS

Belize is tropical and enjoys fairly steady temperatures throughout the year. The average temperature is 79°F (26°C), and the average humidity is about 88 percent. The rainy season is generally from June to November, while the dry season is from late February to May. Rainfall varies across the country and from year to year. Mean annual rainfall per year in the north in Corozal is 60 inches (152 cm), increasing to 74 inches (188 cm) in Belize City, and 175 inches (445 cm) in the south in Punta Gorda.

Belize is vulnerable to storms. Northers are storms that originate in North America and strike Belize with windy, gusty squalls from December to February. Throughout the late summer and fall, Belize is also subject to hurricanes. At the opposite extreme, there is the *mauger* (MAH-ger) season in August when there is no wind at all. The still, oppressive heat can make life miserable for Belizeans, who are also at the mercy of mosquitoes and other insects.

A building has its windows boarded up in preparation for an impending hurricane.

About 8 miles (13 km) north of Half Moon Caye in the middle of Lighthouse Reef is a spectacular geological formation called the Blue Hole. This is a limestone sinkhole, a depression created when the ceiling of a cave beneath the sea collapsed. It is more than 1,000 feet (305 m) across and about 412 feet (126 m) deep, and from the surface appears as a gorgeous dark blue. The Blue Hole was created about 12,000 years ago, and the stalagmites and stalactites present in the caves leading from the Hole indicate that this part of Belize was dry land during the previous Ice Age. Jacques Cousteau, the great French marine explorer, made a documentary about it in 1977, and in 1996 the Belizean government made it part of a 1,023-acre (414 hectares) protected natural monument. It has been designated as a UNESCO World Heritage Site as well.

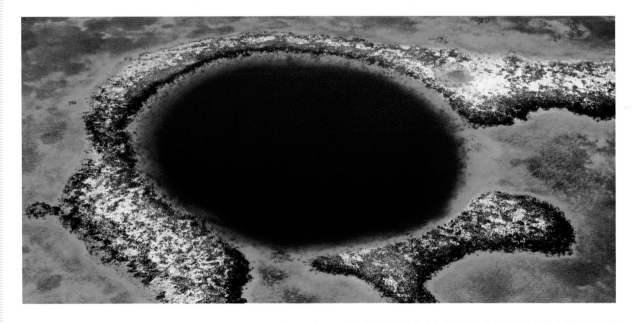

NATURE'S PARADISE

Although pint-size, Belize possesses a very large variety of plants and animals (some unclassified) because it is so sparsely settled and cultivated. Some 72.5 percent of the land is still covered by one or another kind of forest: rain forest, pine forest, mangrove swamp, jungle.

Lily pads line afloat in a protected mangrove backwater.

In the plant kingdom of Belize there are more than 4,000 types of flowering plants, including more than 250 varieties of orchids, 700 kinds of trees, and hundreds of other types of plants. Some of the more interesting trees include the sapodilla, which produces a gum called chicle, an ingredient in chewing gum. The very hard logwood tree was the initial incentive for permanent settlement of Belize, since it produces a purplish-red dye that was extremely important to European textile production from the 16th through the 19th centuries.

Belizean lumberjacks have also harvested mahogany trees. These giant trees can grow up to 150 feet (46 m) tall, spreading to some 20 feet (6 m) across the base. A special type of palm called the cohune palm grows in the interior forests and can reach heights of up to 90 feet (27 m). This bounteous tree provides everything from roofing material (from its fronds) to fuel (from the husk of the nut) to buttons and jewelry (from the nut itself). The meat of the nut can be pounded into flour after the edible oil is extracted. Mangrove trees are found along the coast and on some cays, where saltwater and freshwater intermingle. They can grow to 100 feet (30 m) in height and the abundant prop roots provide habitats for many creatures, including crocodiles, crabs, and manatees. Belize has set aside nearly 20 percent of its mainland mangrove forests within a government protected reserve, whereas more than 90 percent of the world's mangroves have been cut down.

Belize has the third largest reserve of mangroves in the Central American region, surpassed only by Mexico.

Besides an abundance of plant life, Belize is also home to some amazing animals. Two kinds of monkeys can be found in the mainland forests: the howler monkey and the spider monkey. The howler, called "baboon" by the locals, is a large black monkey with powerful arms and shoulders suited to life in the highest reaches of the forest canopy. Howlers get their name from the sounds they make to mark territory and warn off intruders. Other Belizean mammals include the jaguar, jaguarundi, tapir, and dolphin. Baird's tapir, also known as the "mountain cow," is a large herbivorous animal that lives in the highland forests of southern Belize. The national animal of Belize, it is endangered in most of Central America. Although hunting of Baird's tapirs is illegal in Belize, the laws protecting them are often unenforced. Furthermore, hunting restrictions do not address the problems of deforestation. These shy, peaceful mammals forage at night and tend to live alone. They can weigh up to 880 pounds (400 kilograms), but are quite agile in their forest environment. The most famous tapir in Belize, named April, lives in the Belize Zoo. She celebrated her 27th birthday in 2010.

A Baird's tapir is at home in the Belize Zoo.

Apart from mammals, Belize is home to hundreds of bird and reptile species. About 566 known species of birds inhabit Belize. The second-largest flying bird in the Western Hemisphere is the rare jabiru stork with an average wingspan of 10 feet (3 m). There are only 12 nesting pairs known in Belize. Storks are migratory animals, and the jabiru spends summers in Mexico. Other local birds include colorful toucans, macaws, and parrots. Many reptiles live in the waters and jungles of this small country, including the venomous fer-de-lance snake, known locally as the yellow-jawed tommygoff. This is a nocturnal pit viper, equally at home in the cities as in the countryside. This universally feared snake can grow up to 8 feet (2 m) in length and is one of the world's deadliest reptiles. Other reptiles include a variety of turtles and the Yucatecan crocodile, known locally as an "alligator." These animals thrive in mangrove forests and can grow to 12 feet (4 m) in length.

"If the world had any ends, British Honduras (Belize) would certainly be one of them. It is not on the way from anywhere to anywhere else. It has no strategic value. It is all but uninhabited."
—Aldous Huxley, *Beyond the Mexique Bay.*

ALL MANNER OF TURTLES

Belize has become a refuge for some of the world's most endangered species of turtles. Hunted aggressively by men, the Central American river turtle, called hickatee (hik-ah-TEE) locally, is nearly extinct, except in the most remote parts of southern Mexico, northern Guatemala, and Belize. Three other species of sea turtles also use Belizean beaches to lay their eggs: the green, hawksbill, and loggerhead sea turtles.

These turtles have become endangered for a number of reasons. The green turtle has long been hunted to make turtle soup, while the hawksbill's carapace, or shell, was once used extensively to make tortoiseshell frames for eyeglasses, hairbrushes, jewelry, and other decorative items. Trade in tortoiseshell is now outlawed, but the sea turtles remain threatened. Mature females come to shore during the summer to lay their eggs in the sand. By some miracle of nature, these animals find the same beaches where they were born as many as 50 years earlier. Fences, loud noises, dogs, and people, however, all prevent the females from laying their eggs on many beaches. Once the eggs are laid, they are often raided by people who eat them as a delicacy. Those that hatch must then race for the sea at the mercy of birds, crabs, and humans. Only about 5 out of 100 hatchling turtles in each nest make it to the relative safety of seawater.

A COUNTRY WITH TWO CAPITAL CITIES

The biggest and busiest of Belize's cities is Belize City. Approximately 70,800 Belizeans live and work here, making it the most populous city in the country. It is located on the coast where the Belize River empties into the Caribbean Sea. Once the capital of British Honduras, it is the oldest urban settlement in the country. Scottish, English, and French pirates and buccaneers built camps here in the 17th century. Some turned to logging and used the slow-moving Belize River to float logs from the inland forests down to empty ships waiting in the harbor. These camps formed the basis for the development of Belize Town in the 18th and 19th centuries. At only 18 inches (46 cm) above sea level, the city is highly susceptible to flooding in bad weather and is vulnerable to hurricanes off the ocean.

A bird's-eye view of Belize City, the largest city in the country, lies between the Belize River and the Caribbean Sea.

Even before Hurricane Hattie laid to waste 75 percent of Belize City in 1961, there had been talk of moving Belize's capital. Apart from the obvious need to locate government buildings and functions away from the unpredictable fury of the sea, the people living there felt that Belize City was becoming squalid and overcrowded. Construction of a new capital began in 1966 at Belmopan, about 50 miles (80 km) inland from Belize City. The main government complex was designed to look like a Mayan temple, and its name, Belmopan, combines the "Bel" from Belize and "Mopan" from the name of a group of Mayan Indians. The new capital opened officially in 1970, but the expected migration of people out of Belize City did not take place. Even with the growth of Belmopan as a transportation hub, only a few industries have relocated to the new surroundings. In February 2005 the U.S. government broke ground and started building a new U.S. Embassy in Belmopan, 43 years after Belmopan had been chosen as the new capital city. Today, about 16,400 people call Belmopan home. It functions as the national capital, although most commercial activity remains in Belize City.

The shelled fertilized egg requires that the turtles' nests be dug on land; if the eggs were laid in water, the air-breathing embryos would drown.

HISTORY

The Xunantunich ruins in Belize are located on a ridge above the Mopan River. "Xunantunich" (shoo-NAHN-too-nich) means "Stone Woman" in Mayan, after people claimed to have seen the ghost of a woman with fire-red glowing eyes and dressed in white, going up the stone stairs and disappearing into the stone wall.

BELIZE IS THE ONLY COUNTRY IN central America with a British colonial heritage rather than a Spanish one. This difference, which resulted from a number of historical quirks, makes it unique in many ways— it is the only English-speaking nation in Latin America, for example.

At the same time, Belize shares its history with its Spanish-speaking neighbors, since it was also once governed by the Maya, a sophisticated indigenous culture that occupied a vast stretch of territory from southern Mexico to Honduras.

The Caracol ruins are a large, ancient Mayan archaeological site located in the Cayo District of Belize.

The ancient Mayan civilization is believed to have emerged in the lowlands of the Yucatán Peninsula between 2500 B.C. and A.D. 250, spanning parts of modern Mexico, Guatemala, Honduras, and Belize. The cultural legacy of this advanced civilization lives on in preserved archaeological sites such as Cahal Pech, Caracol, Lamanai, Lubaantun, Altun Ha, and Xunantunich.

17

A Maya artisan readies a limestone stela used to record noble events.

BEFORE AND DURING THE MAYAN CIVILIZATION

The original inhabitants of Belize were hunters and gatherers who had crossed the Bering Strait from Asia around 20,000 B.C. and made their way down from Alaska to populate North, Central, and South America. From about 7000 B.C. to 2500 B.C., these nomadic foragers became settled farmers, dependent on corn, beans, and squash for their basic sustenance. By 2500 B.C. the people living in Belize had developed Mayan languages and pottery making. From then until A.D. 250, the preclassic period, the Maya began to acquire the social and agricultural practices that provided the foundation for the classic period of Mayan civilization (A.D. 250 to A.D. 900—1000).

During the classic period Mayan civilization flourished in the Yucatán region of southern Mexico, Guatemala, Belize, and Honduras. Cities were built, some with huge temples and government buildings. Belize treasures the remnants of the earliest Mayan settlements and the late postclassic ceremonial construction, as well as the majestic ruins from the classic period. Cuello, about 3 miles (5 km) west of Orange Walk, is the site of the earliest known Mayan community.

Mayan leaders were thought to possess both human and godly powers. Mayan society consisted of royalty, merchants, and commoners. The merchants were important citizens because they established a commercial network throughout the Mayan lowlands. Products traded among cities included such luxury goods as obsidian—a volcanic glass used for tools and weapons—jade, animal skins, bird feathers, honey, dried fish, cotton, and cacao beans, used in making chocolate.

The Mayans were very sophisticated mathematicians and astronomers. The designers of complex systems of agricultural and water management, they also devised a complicated calendar that combined a 365-day solar

PRE-COLUMBIAN MAYA

Mayan civilization peaked between A.D. 250 and A.D. 900 to 1000, when most of the large ceremonial centers, such as Xunantunich, Altun Ha, and Lamanai, flourished. After this time, archaeological evidence shows a dramatic decline in population and the disappearance of Mayan cities throughout the lowlands of Belize, Guatemala, Honduras, and Mexico.

Mayan specialists have pondered the causes for this rather sudden collapse. A number of explanations have been proposed, including climatic changes, hurricanes, earthquakes, and epidemics of disease. Scholars now believe that the Mayan civilization simply grew too rapidly to feed itself. Relying on tropical agriculture limited how much food could be produced while still allowing the land to recuperate between plantings. It is speculated that the population grew to a point where there were periodic shortages of food, causing malnutrition and starvation, leaving the elite groups incapable of maintaining control. This eventually led to the dispersion of remaining Mayans away from large urban settlements to smaller isolated villages. Although the collapse of the Mayan civilization may have been a quirk of history, some modern scholars think it has relevance for the modern world. Their argument is that humankind may be reproducing beyond our ability to feed ourselves. Perhaps we should study the Mayans more closely to learn from their mistakes.

A range of Mayan glyphs were collected in Mexico, another previous stronghold of the Mayan civilization.

Some scholars have recently theorized that an intense 200-year drought led to the collapse of Mayan civilization. The drought theory arose from research performed by scientists studying lake beds, ancient pollen, and other data.

calendar with a 260-day mystical one. The Mayans calculated the time it takes Venus to go around the sun as 584 days. We now know that it is 583.92 days, so the Mayans were incredibly accurate. They also had an extensive system of hieroglyphic writing with which they recorded their calculations, history, and genealogy.

Near the end of the classic period (A.D. 900), the Mayan civilization lapsed into a decline for generally unknown reasons. Abandoning their cities, most of the Mayans gathered in Guatemala, where they established a refuge and maintained their independence until 1697. Some families continued to live in Belize, and archaeological sites such as those at Cuello, Cerros, Altun Ha, and Lamanai document their enduring presence in the region.

THE EUROPEANS

The Spanish were the first Europeans to arrive in Belize. In the late 15th century they tried to maintain a monopoly of the Caribbean Sea and Central America, leaving Brazil to the Portuguese. While penetrating Belizean forests to cut logwood (used to make dye), they also twice tried to establish Catholic missions among the Mayans in the 17th century, who twice forced them to leave the area. Although the Spanish laid claim to Belize, they did not establish an effective government at that time. Early in the 17th century the Dutch, British, and French arrived on the scene.

British buccaneers established townships along the coast. There were also British settlements on islands off the coast of Honduras and Nicaragua, but in the 1640s the Spanish expelled the preying British from these territories. Some of these British adventurers had used the dangerous coastline of Belize to hide their pirate ships from the Spanish, launching raids from these havens on laden ships headed to Spain. The English moved to the mainland when they were expelled from the Spanish islands. These freebooters, who had originally stolen logwood from the Spanish ships, started to cut and sell it themselves in the 1650s and 1660s. The demand from the European textiles industry for the versatile dye—it could be reddish or bluish, with many variations, depending upon the mordant used and its acidity—obtained from logwood kept the British in the Bay of Honduras for at least a century.

Throughout the 18th century, the Spaniards attacked the British settlements, forcing them to withdraw temporarily. As the Spanish never settled in Belize, the coast was clear for the British to return to harvest logwood and mahogany from its forests. These settlers became known as Baymen (referring to the Bay of Honduras). Through a string of treaties between Spain and England, the Baymen acquired the right to cut wood as far south as the Sibun River, but Spain retained sovereignty over the area, and the British could not farm or govern it. Spain made a final attempt to control the region in 1798 at the Battle of Saint George's Caye but was beaten by the Baymen. Belize was proclaimed a colony of British Honduras in 1862 and a crown colony in 1871.

The independent Mayans, meanwhile, resisted British domination. As the British could not control and organize them as a labor force, they imported African slaves in the early 18th century to cut the marketable wood and perform domestic chores. The British system of slavery was cruel and oppressive, resulting in four slave revolts and hundreds of runaways to the Yucatán Peninsula, Guatemala, and Honduras. Slavery was abolished throughout the British Caribbean in 1838, but the harsh conditions of inequality continued to affect newly freed African Belizeans.

A hand-colored woodcut of caravels. These were light sailing ships, with three or four masts, much used by the Spanish from the 15th to 17th centuries for long voyages.

Until the middle of the 19th century, a small elite group of white Baymen controlled logging, land, and the politics of the settlement of Belize City. These prosperous landowners and businessmen were the only ones allowed to attend the public meetings when decisions were made. If they did not agree with the policies of the Crown representative on duty from England, they could even have him replaced. Ironically, by the 1850s, prices for logwood and mahogany had dropped so far that many of the old Baymen families lost control of their businesses and land. New business speculators from England were able to acquire land and thereby establish a new and powerful class in Belize.

Caribbean slaves in Belize working for the colonial powers.

At the same time, the Clayton—Bulwer Treaty between Britain and the United States had been signed in 1850, stating that Britain would recognize American rights to Central America and withdraw from its colonies there. The Bay Islands of Honduras and the Mosquito Coast in Nicaragua were abandoned by Britain, but because of pressure from London-based businesses, it did not give up Belize, at the time called British Honduras. They created a constitution making it a formal possession of Britain. The new acquisition was not yet a full colony, though it had its own Legislative Assembly. It was also responsible for its own budget and military defense. When groups of Mayans from Mexico arrived in the north in the 1860s and began to farm near logging lands, the new possession funded military expeditions against these usurpers. The Mayans were well organized and even managed to seize Corozal in 1870. As the colony was still in an economic depression, it could not afford these defense costs and thus voted to dissolve the Legislative Assembly, becoming a full Crown Colony of Britain in 1872.

BUCCANEERS, NOT YOUR AVERAGE PIRATES

We often think of buccaneers *as being the same as pirates—murderous maritime thieves of history and legend. The term "buccaneer," however, refers to a special group of people found only in Caribbean history. The word comes from the French words* boucans *and* boucaniers, *which refer to open grills used to roast meat and the people who did the roasting, respectively. The* boucaniers *(or buccaneers as they were called in English) were a group of Europeans (French, English, and Dutch) who made their living hunting wild cattle left behind by the Spanish on the north coast of the island of Hispaniola (modern day Haiti and the Dominican Republic). They preserved the meat by smoking it over grills, and then sold it to passing ships in the early 17th century.*

Since the buccaneers were hostile to Spain and its colonies, in 1640 the Spanish sent in soldiers to drive away the cattle that supplied the settlement on Hispaniola. From that point onward, buccaneer communities sprang up in other parts of the Caribbean, including the Bay Islands of Honduras. English and French governors in the area hired the buccaneers as paid pirates to harass Spanish colonists and ships bound for Europe. One buccaneer, Peter Wallace, was the founder of the first European hamlet in Belize. By the end of the 17th century, Spain and England had signed a peace treaty, and the buccaneers were no longer given formal support. Many turned to real piracy, since they knew how, or found other means of livelihood, such as logging.

A proud sign at the Belize-Guatemala border.

INDEPENDENCE AT LAST

At the end of the 19th century Belize was still largely dependent on forestry. Experiments with other cash crops such as coffee, sugar, and bananas had failed. Belizean-born businessmen and women were forming important ties with American companies and were becoming more influential than the British-born businessmen. For example, in the early 20th century Belize began harvesting chicle for sale to Wrigley's in the United States for the manufacture of their chewing gums. Belize's economy became increasingly dependent on the United States instead of Britain. The Great Depression of the 1930s marked the beginning of the end of British dominance over Belize. During the Depression world prices fell for Belize's main exports, mahogany and chicle, creating unemployment and poverty.

This social upheaval was aggravated by a hurricane in 1931 that destroyed Belize City, leaving most residents homeless. The British government's response to the economic and natural disasters was slow and inadequate. Belizean workers and poor citizens organized themselves politically, forming groups such as the Laborers and Unemployed Association that pushed for reforms in labor law and an awakened political consciousness among Belize's working majority. The People's United Party (PUP) was started in 1950 under the leadership of George Price. The PUP was anti-British and demanded independence. In 1964 British Honduras was granted self-government with a new constitution. When the PUP won the 1965 elections, Price was elected premier. British Honduras was renamed Belize in 1973 and, on September 21, 1981, Belize became a fully independent member of the British Commonwealth of Nations.

CONFLICT WITH GUATEMALA

No history of Belize is complete without a review of the long dispute with Guatemala over the sovereignty of Belizean territory. When the Spanish empire disintegrated in the 1820s, its independent republics claimed sovereign rights over Spain's relinquished territories. Both Mexico and Guatemala made claims on Belize. Mexico dropped its claims in 1893, but Guatemala has persisted with its claims to this day.

A British soldier chats with young children in Belize.

The territorial quarrel was aggravated by a treaty signed in 1859 between Britain and Guatemala. To the British, this treaty simply settled the boundaries of Belize as the area under British dominion; but the Guatemalans would recognize British sovereignty only under certain conditions, the main one being the provision of British aid to build a road from Guatemala City to the Caribbean coast. This road was never built, though, and in 1945 Guatemala adopted a retooled constitution claiming that Belize was the 23rd department of Guatemala. Britain, Guatemala, and Belize have been negotiating this issue ever since, with talks occasionally degenerating into threats of military aggression.

A major turning point came when Belize obtained international support from the United Nations, which paved the way for Belize's independence on September 21, 1981, with the Belize Act, without reaching an agreement with Guatemala. Throughout Belize's entire history, Guatemala has claimed ownership of all or part of the territory. This claim is reflected in some maps showing Belize as a department of Guatemala. The border dispute with Guatemala remains highly contentious, although Guatemala and Belize signed an accord on August 1, 2010, agreeing to let their territorial dispute be settled in the International Court of Justice in The Hague, Netherlands.

"White people but look upon it (Belize) as a resting, not an abiding, place, one from which they hope eventually to return enriched to their native soil."—Archibald Robertson Gibbs, *British Honduras: An Historical and Descriptive Account of the Colony from Its Settlement 1883.*

GOVERNMENT

The courthouse in Belize city.

BELIZE'S HISTORY AS AN independent nation is short, dating back only to 1981. The structure of its government is based on the British parliamentary system, and its legal system is based on the common law system in England. The Queen of England is the head of state.

A placard protests the ongoing Guatemalan claims on Belizean land.

Belize's most pressing foreign concern has been neighboring Guatemala's claim to its territory. This issue arose from imperial Spain's colonization of the region during the late 15th century and was aggravated by the 1859 British-Guatemalan treaty. Mediated negotiations since then have been unsuccessful, with border relations strained by the disagreements.

Parliament of
Belize in the
capital, Belmopan.

STRUCTURES OF GOVERNMENT

The first constitution of 1981 established Belize as a constitutional monarchy, which means that the Queen of England, currently Elizabeth II, is recognized as the nominal head of state. Her representative in Belize is the governor-general, a Belizean national whose functions are mainly ceremonial. The current governor-general is Sir Colville N. Young.

The effective leader of Belize is the prime minister, who is the head of the party that wins a majority in the House of Representatives. The governor-general appoints the prime minister, based on the outcome of elections. The prime minister then appoints the cabinet. There are 31 seats in the House, and these are divided into constituencies based on population and are divided among Belize's six districts. In addition to the House of Representatives, there is a 12-member Senate. Of these 12 senators, 6 are appointed by the prime minister, 3 by the leader of the opposition party, 1 by the Belize Council of Churches and the Evangelical Association of Churches, 1 by the Belize Chamber of Commerce and Industry and the Belize Business Bureau, and 1 by the National Trade Union Congress of Belize and the Civil Society Steering Committee.

Bills are proposed by the prime minister and his or her cabinet. Cabinet members act as ministers, and can be drawn from either the House or the Senate. There are 19 ministries in Belize today, dealing with all the following: Agriculture and Fisheries; Budget Planning and Management; Economic Development; Education and Sports; Finance; Foreign Affairs; Health; Housing and Urban Development; Human Development, Women and Youth; Industry and Commerce; Investment and Trade; National Security and Immigration; Natural Resources and the Environment; Public Services and Labour; Public Utilities, Transport and Communication; Rural Development and Culture; Sugar Industry, Local Government and Latin American Affairs; Tourism; Works. When the cabinet passes a bill with a majority vote, it is sent to the Senate to be ratified in another vote. The last step is for the governor-general to sign the bill into law. The government is formed for a maximum of 5 years, though the same prime minister can be elected for more than one term.

The city hall in Belize City.

There are Summary Jurisdiction Courts for criminal cases and District Courts for civil cases in each of Belize's six districts. Appeals can first be taken to the Supreme Court, which is independent of the national government. After a Supreme Court decision, there is a possibility for appeal in the Court of Appeal. Absolute authority rests with the Privy Council in England. The governor-general, in consultation with the prime minister, appoints justices to the Supreme Court, but they are expected to remain neutral and avoid party politics. A special Family Court has been set up to hear specific cases regarding child maintenance, domestic violence, spousal abuse and other similar cases. A Quick Trial Court processes selected cases especially fast.

In addition to the national government, there are also elected town boards with seven members for each district. Belize City has a nine-member City Council, and the towns of San Pedro and Benque Viejo del Carmen also have their own boards. Local elections are held every 3 years. These municipal governments work with village councils and are funded by property taxes, trade licenses, and national government grants. Some Mayan villages also have a mayor, with limited powers, however.

The San Ignacio police headquarters.

MILITARY AND POLICE

A British army team arriving to assist at the Belize Jungle School.

The Belizean Defense Force (BDF), formed in 1978, consists of about 1,000 soldiers, 50 marines, and a 15-member air wing. Until 1989 the BDF was under the command of a British officer. In 1989 a Belizean officer was appointed to head the BDF for the first time in Belize's short history as an independent country. The BDF, currently under the command of General Dario Tapia, assumed total defense responsibility from British Forces Belize (BFB) on January 1, 1994. In 1995 the Ministry of National Security was created to advise the government on national security matters. The United Kingdom continues to maintain the British Army Training Support Unit Belize (BATSUB) to assist in the administration of the Belize Jungle School. The BDF receives military assistance from both the United States and the United Kingdom.

Local policing is done by the Belize Police Force (BPF), which has about 1,200 police officers posted throughout all six districts. The murder rate in Belize has increased, primarily because of unsolved gang-related issues and the availability of drugs on the streets. Recently the BDF and BPF have been cooperating to fight urban crime and drug smuggling, two of the most serious internal defense problems.

A People's United Party (PUP) election board in San Pedro on Ambergris Cay.

In a diverse country of indigenous Mayans, mestizos, and African-descended Creoles and Garifuna, many on the street rejoiced at the Creole Dean Barrow's winning national power. Belize's past leaders had been born in Belize but were of European descent.

POLITICAL PARTIES

There are two main political parties in Belize, the People's United Party (PUP) and the United Democratic Party (UDP). Between them, they have controlled the government since the start of self-government and the formation of the Legislative Assembly in 1964. The PUP, the first political party in Belize, was formed in 1950 to represent those who wanted independence from Britain. Originally it relied on the support of labor, but since 1964 it has broadened its base to include Belizeans of all classes. Generally the PUP is the more right wing of the two main parties. Under the leadership of George Cadle Price, it won every election since independence in 1981 except twice (1984 and 1993), but massive discontent with the PUP in 2005, including tax increases in the national budget, led to a landslide victory for the UDP in the 2008 elections. The UDP won 25 out of the 31 seats in the House of Representatives, and on February 8, 2008, Dean Barrow of the UDP was sworn in as Belize's first black prime minister. The *Belize Times* is the official newspaper of the PUP, and also is the longest continuously published newspaper in Belize since 1950.

The UDP was formed in 1973 as a combination of three existing political parties: the National Independence Party, the People's Development Movement, and the Liberal Party. By the time the UDP won its first election in 1984, under the leadership of Manuel Esquivel, they had hammered out a comprehensive platform, including support for foreign investment and private sector solutions to economic problems. This was a significant election as Manuel Esquivel replaced George Cadle Price as Belize's second prime minister. The UDP's official newspaper is the *Guardian*. In 1989 the UDP lost the elections to the PUP, but won again in 1993. In the 1998 general elections, the party suffered a disaster, winning only three seats. PUP leader Said Musa was the prime minister from August 28, 1998, to February 8, 2008. The UDP is currently the ruling party following the 2008 watershed elections.

All classes of people and regions of the country support both the parties. Belizeans may choose which party to vote for based on their family traditions or on locally important current issues, but they do not choose between radically differing political platforms.

GEORGE PRICE, FATHER OF THE NATION

George Cadle Price, shown at right, below, is Belize's George Washington. From a middle-class background, he was educated at Belize's elite secondary school, Saint John's College. His first choice of career was the Roman Catholic Church, and he studied with the Jesuits in the United States in the 1930s. When he returned to Belize in 1942, he worked closely with Robert Turton, the Creole chicle millionaire, who was an elected member of the Legislative Council at that time. Price was inspired to enter politics and won a seat on the Belize City Council in 1947. A central figure in national politics ever since, he formed the People's United Party (PUP) in 1950 and led Belize's independence movement. He was often criticized for maintaining total control of the PUP but was also highly regarded for his honesty, integrity, and incorruptibility. He is considered as the Father of the Nation as he was the man in power when Belize gained internal control of the government in 1964 and total independence in 1981.

George Price, currently in his 90s, is an eclectic and pragmatic politician, holding on to his preeminent position longer than any other national leader in the region.

OLD SYMBOLS FOR A NEW NATION

The flag of Belize honors its history as an English protectorate and as a wood-producing country. The center of the dark blue flag portrays the coat of arms of British Honduras, granted by royal warrant in 1907. The shield of the coat of arms is divided into three parts: the left side contains a squaring ax and paddle crossed; the right side contains a beating ax and saw crossed; and the bottom shows a ship in full sail. The axes and saw represent the tools used to harvest timber, and the paddle and ship indicate the way that the logs were taken from the interior down the rivers to the coast and then shipped across the Atlantic Ocean to England. On either side of the shield stand two woodcutters, one holding an ax and one holding a paddle for boats. Behind the shield is the crest and a mahogany tree, and below the shield is the motto in Latin: Sub Umbra Floreo *(Under the Shade I Flourish). A wreath encircles the coat of arms.*

CURRENT POLITICS AND NEW LEADERS

Dean Oliver Barrow, the current prime minister of Belize, is also the leader of the United Democratic Party. A practicing attorney, he served as deputy prime minister and minister of foreign affairs from 1993 to 1998 and was the Leader of the Opposition until the UDP won the February 2008 election. He is also considered one of Belize's most successful attorneys and has appeared in several high profile cases. From 1993 to 1998, when the UDP was ruling Belize, Barrow's critics dubbed him "Minister of Everything" during this period because he appeared at most major functions on behalf of the UDP government. After the 1998 election loss he was elected leader of the UDP. In the 2008 elections Barrow ran on a platform of ridding Belize of the embezzlement scandals and financial mismanagement that battered Said Musa's last years in office. Since his confirmation as prime minister, Barrow has also appointed himself minister of finance. He plans to get more Belizeans to invest in the tourism industry, which, despite the country's lush jungles and sparkling coral reefs, lags behind its neighbors Costa Rica and Mexico.

A big issue facing Prime Minister Dean Oliver Barrow is Belize's $1 billion debt. About 25 percent of government spending goes to pay down debt.

Prime Minister of Belize, Dean Oliver Barrow is also the leader of the United Democratic Party and an attorney by trade.

ECONOMY

Townspeople waiting for the bank to open in Punta Gorda.

CHAPTER 4

BELIZE HAS A SMALL, ESSENTIALLY private enterprise economy that is based primarily on agriculture, agro-based industry, and merchandising. Tourism has become the number one foreign exchange earner, and construction has recently assumed greater importance.

Moreover, Belize has become a service economy with 54.1 percent of its gross domestic product (GDP) and more than 74 percent of workers employed in tourism, construction, banking, communications, transportation, and community services.

Bottles of hot pepper sauce are inspected and packed at a factory in Dangriga.

With a small, mostly private-enterprise economy, tourism and exports form the backbone of Belize's economy. Although successful policies had helped to boost the country's GDP growth, the recession and natural disasters were hurdles in overcoming the heavy trade deficits.

Such illegal drugs as marijuana are grown in Belize for export to the United States. Most industry is based on agriculture, like flour milling, the production of citrus concentrates, and animal feed. A small industrial sector produces goods for local consumption, such as beer, cigarettes, soft drinks, furniture, and construction materials.

FORESTRY AND AGRICULTURE

The sale of timber abroad has been the basis of the Belizean economy for many years, but today forest products are more in demand by Belizeans themselves. Forest products such as furniture, chewing gum, and electric power and telephone poles are made from mahogany logs, chicle, and pine lumber.

Sugarcane being transported for processing in Belize City.

Since the 1970s, agricultural products, particularly sugar and bananas, have been the leading export earners of foreign currencies for Belize. Agriculture engages 22.5 percent of the population. Sugarcane is grown in the districts of Corozal and Orange Walk, and Belize exports sugar to the United States and to markets in the European Union. Other exports include bananas, citrus fruits (oranges, pomelos, and grapefruit), crude oil, and seafood products. Citrus fruits and bananas are grown mainly in the Stann Creek and Cayo areas, south and west of Belize City. Bananas are grown in the southern regions of Stann Creek and Toledo, the outcome of a government initiative in the early 1970s to improve export earnings and relieve poverty in this struggling region. Rice also is grown in Toledo District.

A grove of citrus fruit was called a "walk" in Belize, giving rise to the name of a district and town, Orange Walk.

Large companies who employ thousands of Belizeans, as permanent, temporary, or seasonal workers, own most of the farms growing high-income-earning products for export such as sugar, citrus fruits, and bananas. There are 59,000 acres (23,877 ha) of land planted in sugarcane in northern Belize (Corozal and Orange Walk) owned by 5,000 farmers. In 1981 an estimated 30 percent of farmland, formerly used for growing sugarcane, had been abandoned as it was no longer usable because of monocultural soil depletion.

Laborers waiting to be chosen for underpaid, often abusive, farm jobs near the Southern Highway.

Another 40,000 acres (16,188 ha) is under citrus fruit cultivation. In the early 1990s citrus production was controlled by two processing companies, the Citrus Company of Belize and Nestlé. Hummingbird Hershey Company, a part of Hershey Foods Corporation, started a small cacao plantation in 1977, and it also buys some cacao from local, small-scale farmers. Other products, such as peanuts, mangoes, and pawpaws, are currently being test-marketed as profitable export crops by the Belizean government.

Belizeans also produce food for their own consumption. The two main crops are rice and kidney beans. Belize exports beans, but it has to import rice. Other locally produced and consumed products include beef, pork, chicken, milk, eggs, and corn. Belize is self-sufficient in milk and chicken, largely because of the efforts of the German immigrant Mennonite communities, which have improved local agricultural practices.

About 10 percent of adult Belizeans work in agriculture either as poorly paid farm laborers or as small, independent farmers. Many work on sugarcane plantations. Cutting sugarcane is one of the worst jobs in the world, since the cane fields are full of snakes and rats, and the leaves on the canes are razor sharp. Citrus fruit pickers, too, are generally underpaid and abused by employers. Nevertheless, vulnerable workers step up to fill these miserable jobs.

FISHING

Belize's main marine exports are shrimp, lobster tails, and conch. Fishermen are organized into cooperatives in Belize, which means they get more of the profits than if they were employed by a big company. The cooperatives are given exclusive rights to harvest the sea, and because every fisherman is also an owner of the cooperative, he earns a higher price for his catch. Unfortunately, there has been a decline in the number of exportable fish because of overfishing in the past 20 years. In 2000 the Fisheries Act was passed to protect Belize's diminishing stock of fish.

Fishermen comparing their catches in Lamanai.

The Rio Bravo Conservation and Management Area is the largest private reserve in Belize and protects extensive areas of various habitats. More than 70 mammal species, 390 bird species, and 22 flora types have been recorded in this reserve.

In the early 1990s Belize began to farm shrimp rather than relying on trawling in the sea. Farmed shrimp has become an important income earner, although it has a negative environmental impact, as the farms are built in deliberately destroyed mangrove forest areas. The World Wildlife Fund (WWF) has named shrimp aquaculture as one of the largest threats to the Mesoamerican Reef. Hopefully, the fishing cooperatives will find a way to diversify or to allow the lobster and conch time to replenish their numbers.

TOURISM

A combination of natural factors supports the thriving tourism and ecotourism industry—climate; the Belize Barrier Reef (longest in the Western Hemisphere); 127 offshore cays; excellent fishing; safe water for boating, scuba diving, and snorkeling; numerous rivers for rafting and kayaking; various jungle and wildlife reserves of fauna and flora for hiking and bird-watching; and helicopter touring, as well as many treasured Mayan ruins.

FROM PLANTATION TO ENVIRONMENTAL RESERVE

Rio Bravo Conservation and Management Area is a nature reserve located in northwestern Belize. Rio Bravo, as it is known, was established by Program for Belize, a nonprofit Belizean organization, in 1988 with the purchase of 110,044 acres (44,533 ha) of land from Gallon Jug Agroindustries. With logging encroachment imminent in 1989, the Nature Conservancy joined Program for Belize to protect the land. Additional land donations from Coca-Cola Foods, Inc.—42,007 acres (17,000 ha) in 1990 and 52,015 acres (21,050 ha) in 1992—and purchases from New River Enterprises Ltd.—14,011 acres (5,670 ha) and 12,798 acres (5,179 ha)—both in 1994—enlarged the protected area to 230,875 acres (93,435 ha).

Rio Bravo, the largest terrestrial conservation area in Belize, encompasses 4 percent of the country's total land area. The reserve has continued to operate, depending on private contributions, many of which are channeled through the Massachusetts Audubon Society. The reserve is managed by Program for Belize and is among many busy tourist sites. This is a good example of how Belizeans and outsiders cooperate to preserve the country's natural environment.

Development costs are high, but they pay off handsomely, as tourism is now the number one foreign exchange earner. In 2007 tourist arrivals totalled 251,655 (more than 210,000 from the United States), and tourist revenue amounted to $183.3 million. The tourism industry is an important part of the economy of Belize, in 2007 contributing more than 25 percent of all jobs and making up more than 18 percent of the GDP. One in every four jobs today is in the tourism industry.

CURRENCY AND CRIME

Belize's official currency is the Belize dollar, which for many years has been pegged to the U.S. dollar at a rate of 2 Belize dollars to 1 U.S. dollar. Moneychangers often give a slightly higher rate than 2 Belize for 1 U.S. dollar, however, sometimes at 2.2 to 1 or higher, depending on the local demand for American greenbacks. Businesses in Belize routinely take U.S. dollars in payment for goods and services, standard practice for decades.

An antidrug billboard in Dangriga proclaims a stark fact.

ECOTOURS AND ECOEXPORTS

One of Belize's most productive income earners is tourism. If Belize's beautiful forests and its reefs—the main attractions for tourists and the habitats for an unrivalled variety of wildlife—are destroyed, one of the country's most important industries will disappear.

The Belize Ecotourism Association (BETA) was created on Earth Day in 1993 to promote environmentally responsible tourism—ecotourism, which emphasizes the protection of natural environments and the safekeeping of local cultures. Another sound effort is the harvesting of natural products without the felling of trees. Both Belizean and foreign-owned companies have started this practice and export only ecologically and environmentally friendly products from the rain forest, such as natural chewing gum from chicle, cashew candy, dried jungle fruits, coconut soap, and cohune nut jewelry and buttons. An inherent benefit of this new practice is that local residents are usually employed to do the harvesting and crafting.

Very harmful to Belizeans is the illegal trade in drugs. In the 1980s Belize became a producer and exporter of marijuana. The United States Drug Enforcement Administration (DEA) underwrote programs to spray marijuana fields with pesticides, and by the end of the 1980s far less marijuana was being produced. An ominous new problem emerging in the 1990s was cocaine and its by-product, crack. The Belize Defense Force reported that it had destroyed close to 150,000 marijuana plants and almost a ton of compressed marijuana in the north and south of the country in the first four months of 2010. Despite its reputation as a primary source of marijuana and, recently, as a transhipment point for cocaine and other drugs from South America, Belize has strict laws on the use of illegal drugs, with prison terms and fines for offenders. Quite a few Belizeans smoke marijuana, some fairly openly, but it is nonetheless illegal. Unfortunately, crack, heroin, and other hard drugs are a fact of life in Belize, as they are in many countries. A large share of the crime in Belize City and other parts of the country is tied to drugs.

Shipping containers filled with cacao beans form a cubistic cityscape in the port of San Pedro.

TRADE

As a small country, Belize must rely on preferential trade agreements in order to compete with larger producers in regional markets. World commodity price fluctuations and continuation of preferential trading agreements, especially with the United States, the European Union (EU), and the United Kingdom (UK), greatly impact Belize's economic performance. For example, the United States buys a percentage of Belizean sugar at a price much higher than that on the open market. U.S. trade preferences that allow duty-free shipments have significantly expanded the apparel industry. Preferences by the EU and UK also have been vital for the growth and prosperity of those industries.

With its small manufacturing base, Belize must import much of its clothing and appliances, as well as transportation and other equipment. Belize also imports food, industrial chemicals, petroleum, and beverages. As a result, the cost of living is higher in Belize than in neighboring countries.

Belize's economic performance is highly susceptible to foreign market ups and downs, a fact that was reflected in the rise of its real growth rate from 1.2 percent in 2007 to 2.1 percent in 2008. The global slowdown hit Belize hard, and in 2009 growth fell to -1.5 percent. Belize continues to rely heavily on foreign trade. Imports as of June 2009 totaled $616 million, while total exports were $395 million. The United States continues to be Belize's number one trading partner. Through 2009 the United States provided 38 percent of all Belizean imports and took in 37 percent of Belize's total exports. Other major trading partners include Mexico, the United Kingdom, the European Union, Central American nations, and the Caribbean Community (CARICOM) member states. In 2006 to 2007, Taiwan and Japan emerged as new trading partners with Belize.

Workers sorting oranges in a citrus processing facility. Citrus production is one of the main agricultural industries in Belize.

The Philip Goldson International Airport and control tower near Belize City in Ladyville.

TRANSPORTATION

Since the decline of forestry in the 1950s, roads have become more important. Whereas loggers could use rivers to float their products to the ports and international markets, sugar and citrus growers needed roads to truck their goods to markets and ports. The first paved road connected Belize City with the Mexican border in the north and is called, appropriately, the Northern Highway. Next to be built was the Western Highway that connects Belize City and Belmopan with Benque Viejo del Carmen on the Guatemalan border. More recently, the Hummingbird Highway from Belmopan to Dangriga was constructed, followed by a new Southern Highway from Dangriga to Punta Gorda. By 2006 there was a total of 1,868 miles (3,006 km) of roads in Belize, of which only 357 miles (575 km) were paved.

With the help of foreign aid, the main airport, the Philip Goldson International Airport, was expanded and renovated in 1990. The airport is now going through major renovations such as lengthening of the runway, widening the apron, and enlarging the terminal. These improvements are being made mainly to handle more planes and to be able to bring in flights from Europe. They are expected to be completed by 2015.

The Port of Belize is the largest port in the country. There are two other main commercial ports—Big Creek Port is primarily used for banana exports, while Commerce Bight Port is mostly used for citrus fruit exports—and several smaller ports.

TELECOMMUNICATIONS

Belize was among the first Latin American countries to privatize its national telecom company in 1988, but it gave the incumbent, Belize Telecommunications Ltd. (BTL), a 15-year monopoly concession until end of 2002 for all fixed-line and mobile phone services. In May 2007 the company changed its name from Belize Telecommunications Ltd. to Belize Telemedia Ltd. The company was nationalized in August 2009 by the government, which bought more than 94 percent of its shares.

ENERGY

As of 2003, 71 percent of Belize's energy was imported, while only 29 percent of its energy was produced domestically. Mexico supplies 50 percent of the imported energy. The energy comes from four main sources: imported fossil fuels, 66 percent; biomass, 26 percent; hydroelectricity, 3 percent; and imported electricity, 5 percent. In 2006 a newly discovered crude-oil field near the town of Spanish Lookout gave Belize a tiny domestic oil industry. Oil production is currently 3,000 barrels a day, and oil exports are 1,960 barrels a day. Belize's energy needs are projected to grow at 9 percent annually, which makes the use of alternative energy sources an urgent step for the country.

In 1991 all taxes on imported solar and wind energy generating devices were revoked to encourage people to install and use alternative sources of energy. The sugar industry in Belize has used its by-product, bagasse (juiced-out canes), to provide the energy for powering its own factories, making sugar production carbon neutral. In early 2010 the Belize Hydroelectric Company was ordered by the Forest Department of Belize to "cease and desist" all activities in the Bladen Nature Reserve, because of its illegal harvesting of the forest.

A swing bridge takes both pedestrians and vehicles across a creek in Belize City.

ENVIRONMENT

The clear tropical waters of Goff's Caye in Caye Caulker.

BELIZE HAS BECOME ONE OF THE world's most biologically diverse nations, with the integrity of its natural resources still very much intact. It extols the 72.5 percent of its land that lies under forest covers, the largest coral reef in the Western Hemisphere (second only to Australia's), the largest cave system in Central America, more than 500 species of birds, thousands of Mayan archaeological temples and related structures, and the only jaguar reserve in the world.

The government-appointed Ministry of Tourism and the Environment is responsible for regulating and protecting the environment in Belize. Major non-governmental environmental organizations and conservation groups include the Belize Audubon Society (BAS), the Belize Zoo and Tropical Education Center (TEC), the Monkey Bay Wildlife Sanctuary, and the Wildlife Conservation International (WCI).

Banded butterfly fish swimming in the colorful barrier reef made of various corals and algae found off San Pedro.

A water catchment system on wooden stilts provides this beach home in Caye Caulker with precious fresh water.

To ensure proper financial backing, the Protected Areas Conservation Trust (PACT) was created. This trust is responsible for all fund-raising, and the delegation of monetary aid to protected areas.

With only 8,867 square miles (22,966 square km) and 314,522 people, the population density is the lowest in the Central American region and one of the lowest in the world. Since Belize declared its independence in 1981, the government has passed many environmental protection acts that have had a profound influence on the conservation of biodiversity in the country. These acts have established many different types of protected areas, with each category having its own set of rules regarding everything from public access and large-scale resource extraction to the small-scale harvest of animals and plants for local populations and to general tourism behavior. The success of these parks has played a large part in keeping roughly 40 percent of the country protected and conserved.

CONSERVATION LAWS AND ORGANIZATIONS

Belize always had environmental laws and regulations in the past, but they were relatively relaxed and unenforced. With the formation of the Belize Audubon Society in 1973, however, awareness regarding environmental protection grew rapidly. By the time Belize achieved independence, the country had received an important education related to the value of protected lands for the good of the environment and the country. That same year both the National Parks System Act and the Wildlife Protection Act were passed, designating many protected areas of different status, as well as the protection of the immense biodiversity of life contained in the parks.

Following soon after was the Environmental Protection Act of 1992, which outlined the statutory powers of the Department of the Environment.

WATER USE IN BELIZE

Domestic water consumption in Belize is at about the same proportionate amounts as is consumed in industrialized countries. Surface water makes up about 70 percent of the total water used in urban areas. Groundwater from wells and springs is also used as a source of drinking water in the cities of the Corozal, Orange Walk, Cayo, and Toledo districts and in some rural areas of Toledo and Cayo. Data on water sources used by industry are not available. It is assumed, however, that surface water is also its main water source. The amount of water used for irrigation is estimated to be less than 1 percent of the total water withdrawn.

Water quality in urban areas is good and is constantly monitored by the Water and Sewerage Authority (WASA). In rural areas, however, the water quality, mainly in the districts of Toledo, Stann Creek, and Cayo, is not satisfactory: full water purification takes place only in the systems that are connected to urban WASA systems (about 30 percent).

About half the rural population is without clean water. The barrier reef and its animal and plant life are threatened by water pollution, the removal of coral, and spearfishing.

Children collecting water at the Laguna village pump.

POLLUTION IN AMBERGRIS CAYE

Trash and other pollutants are found on the beaches in Belize.

Ambergris Caye, which was once a stable, quiet fishing village, today has become one of the most popular tourist destinations of the Caribbean. With this change in the population of the island, the dynamics of the local environment have also been altered. The increased population of San Pedro, the only town on the island, as well as the flood of tourists, has caused the environment in and around Ambergris Caye to be increasingly impacted by pollution.

Pollution, such as an oil spill, is introduced to the coastal area via small boats or passing cruise ships. In 1990 many gallons of diesel fuel spilled into San Pedro Harbor. When a spill occurs, the toxic portion of the oil is either ingested or absorbed by marine creatures, especially by invertebrates that often die from it. The heavier portion of the oil sinks to the sea floor, blanketing slow-moving or stationary animals such as corals and sponges. Humans who may consume animals that have been contaminated by oil also face threatening toxicity.

Water in San Pedro is also polluted by domestic sewage originating from toilets, washing machines, kitchens, and other domestic sources. Not only does sewage pose a threat to human health but it also is harmful to local plants and animals. Because of the large amounts of nitrates and phosphates in sewage, the water can be overenriched, which leads to the overproduction of microscopic organisms that can kill coral and other plants and animals. Today, some but not all of San Pedro residences are equipped with septic systems, instead of being connected to sewers, thus decreasing the presence of polluted water.

These are only a few sources of pollution affecting the environment of San Pedro. Other pollutants include solid wastes (trash), agrochemicals, and industrial effluents.

DEFORESTATION

Deforestation has been a major problem in Belize and is still increasing. A study conducted by Sonia DiFiore, a conservation coordinator of the Cleveland Zoological Society, showed that over an 11-year period, 11 percent of the forest of Belize disappeared. This can lead to many issues, such as erosion, and affects the main sources of freshwater in Belize. These problems could be devastating for all the wildlife that lives in Belize. The people and the wildlife together depend on the ground cover and the rivers as main sources of life.

WASTE TREATMENT AND DISPOSAL

Belizean refuse-removal by-laws prohibit littering and the indiscriminate dumping of waste in public places. These regulations require the occupants of each premise to provide a suitable receptacle for containing household refuse—a garbage can. The Public Health Act deals with liquid and solid waste disposal and other issues relating to public health in general. The Ministry of Health is mandated to address public health issues and related complaints, the monitoring of sewage and solid waste, and the prosecution of offenders. Town and village boards are generally responsible for solid waste management in their jurisdictional areas.

CORAL BLEACHING OF THE BELIZE BARRIER REEF

Scientists say rising ocean temperatures, increased exposure to ultraviolet radiation, more frequent and violent storms, and weather patterns possibly caused by global climate change have led to a partial die-off of the Belize coral reef. This is known as coral bleaching. The Belize reef is unique, for Belize is sparsely populated and the effect of human activity on the reef is a lot less than in densely populated countries such as Jamaica, yet it is starting to bleach and die off, a disturbing glimpse of what lies ahead.

Coral bleaching—a type of slow death evident when multihued coral reefs turn a ghostly translucent white—is relatively new to Belize. The first mass bleaching occurred in 1995, with an estimated partial mortality of 10 percent of coral colonies, according to the Coastal Zone Management Institute.

In 1997 and 1998 a second mass bleaching event occurred, coinciding with devastation wreaked by hurricane Mitch. Marine biologists observed a 48 percent reduction in live coral cover in the Belize reef system. In the past, scientists often attributed bleaching events to local causes: storms, sedimentation, and pollution. But when bleaching began to occur in more remote reefs like Belize, scientists began to reevaluate their assumptions.

"This coral bleaching is pretty solidly tied to rising ocean temperatures," said Melanie McField, a Belize-based reef scientist with the World Wildlife Fund, a nonprofit environmental organization in Washington, D.C. "It is a fact that global temperatures have risen. There are lots of data and little argument that the increased ocean temperatures are the primary agents of bleaching. Ultraviolet light also causes bleaching, and the combination of the two gives you the worst bleaching response." The problems of the reefs will multiply as global climate change models predict that ocean temperatures will continue to rise in the foreseeable future.

Corals often survive infrequent bleaching, but recovery is a slow process during which corals are vulnerable to other threats. Diseases will attack coral reefs that are only slightly damaged.

In areas of Belize waters where live coral cover has died, there is still a chance for recovery. Large-scale algae cover, which often overwhelms dying reefs, has not occurred widely. This gives biologists hope that the work of other ecosystem factors, such as relatively healthy algae-eating fish populations, may give the coral time to recover.

For Belize to combat such a gargantuan opponent as global warming, all efforts to better identify the characteristics that make reefs resistant to coral bleaching are critical. It is known that higher current flows cool reefs and wash away the toxic products of cellular processes, and that even more resistant coral species can stave off bleaching. To save this vital area of the country and of Planet Earth, Belize must do all it can—starting now.

SEWAGE TREATMENT

In Belize City sewage treatment facilities consist of two authorized lagoons situated south of the city. The lagoon tanks operate in series and are designed to provide 10 days of hydraulic retention time each for the sewage, although the actual retention time could be doubled in the dry season. Treated effluent is discharged from the lagoon tanks into canals that cut through a mangrove wetlands, which discharges into the Sibun Bight, a body of water next to the coastline. Early problems in the lagoons included premature corrosion of the tanks and weed growth. Now, however, the lagoons are generally in good condition, providing some 80 to 85 percent effectiveness.

In Belmopan the treatment involves sedimentation tanks only, with the effluent discharging into the Belize River. Not all the meters and pumps are working, and the treatment plant is partly bypassed, resulting in an effectiveness of about only 5 percent. Currently, the plant is a potential health hazard because of fecal contamination of the Belize River.

The Mountain Pine Ridge Forest Reserve in Cayo District of Belize helps to preserve various species of plant life.

The Belize Recycling Company also gathers up old cars free of charge, so the people of Belize have a service to remove ugly metal eyesores from their yards.

RECYCLING

The Belize Recycling Company opened its doors in 2005 and buys used paper from individuals and businesses or has it donated from the public. The manager said that in a month they collect approximately 28 to 30 tons of paper. Cardboard adds about 8 to 10 tons. From their downtown depot the paper is sent to another location, where it is separated and packaged. Most of the paper is then shipped in containers to a processor in Guatemala, which renders the scrap into new paper products. Some of that trash paper, however, finds its way to the Caribbean Paper Company on the Western Highway, from which it is shipped to conversion plants. Machines at the conversion plants, some of which are located in Guatemala, El Salvador, and Mexico, reduce the paper to pulp, which is cleaned, kneaded, and bleached if necessary. The newly recycled paper is then shipped back to Belize in gigantic rolls. At the Caribbean Paper warehouse, the huge rolls are converted into napkins, paper towels, and toilet paper, which is marketed under the brand names Softy, Elite, and Class.

The Belize Recycling Company also collects many different scrap metals. They pack the metals for export in flatbed trucks. A loaded flatbed may contain 80 percent iron and 20 percent other metals, such as aluminium, copper, and bronze.

PLANTS

Belize has one of the world's richest habitats for flora. No fewer than 4,000 different species of native flowering plants are found within its borders, along with several hundred species of other plants. Scientists only now are beginning to carry out an exhaustive inventory of Belize's plants. The task is daunting: more than 70 percent of the country is under some kind of forest cover, and almost half of Belize's primary forest is still standing.

TREES

Belizean forests support more than 700 tree species, including a large variety of economically and historically important trees. Commercially valuable trees have played a vital role in the history of the country. Indeed, the very existence of Belize as a colony are inseparable from the logging industry. The most important historical tree crops have been logwood, mahogany, and chicle, and they are still heavy earners today. The national tree of Belize is the mahogany tree.

Close-up of a manatee in the crystal-clear waters of Belize.

ENDANGERED ANIMALS

In Belize, the coastal species described below are considered endangered, threatened, or vulnerable by the Convention on International Trade in Endangered Species (CITES). The primary cause for their endangered status is the loss of habitat, including nesting sites.

CROCODILES There are two crocodile species in Belize, both endangered: the American saltwater crocodile and the Morelet's crocodile. Reasons for their endangered status include loss of habitat, being killed as pests, and being hunted for their meat and hides.

MANATEES An unusual attraction for tourists, Belize's population of manatees is estimated to number between 300 and 700 individuals. The major threats to manatees are poaching for their meat, collision with boats, entanglement in fishing nets, and loss of feeding habitats.

The national flower of Belize is the black orchid (*Encyclia cochleatum*). There are approximately 250 species of orchids in Belize.

CATS There are five wildcat species in Belize. The jaguar, the largest, was one of the most revered animals of the ancient Maya and even today commands great respect among Belizeans. Alan Rabinowitz, author of *Jaguar: One Man's Struggle to Establish the World's First Jaguar Preserve*, during an intensive field study, brought the jaguar into the international spotlight as a means of protecting the Cockscomb Basin Wildlife Sanctuary and Jaguar Reserve, the only designated jaguar preserve in the world. The other four native cats of Belize are the puma, ocelot, margay, and jaguarundi.

NATIONAL PARKS AND RESERVES

COCKSCOMB BASIN WILDLIFE SANCTUARY AND JAGUAR RESERVE Belize's jaguar reserve, established in 1984, is a wildlife sanctuary etched in the middle of the jungle south of Dangriga. Situated amid the shadows of the Maya Mountains, the sanctuary encompasses some 100,000 acres (40,470 ha) of tropical forest that rises from 300 feet (91 m) above sea level to approximately 3,675 feet (1,120 m) at the summit of Victoria Peak. The sanctuary is home to numerous members of the cat family, and there is also a large population of other mammals and birds to support the food chain.

The majestic jaguars are protected in Belize's unique jaguar reserve.

COMMUNITY BABOON SANCTUARY This baboon sanctuary on the banks of the Belize River is situated some 30 miles (48 km) west of Belize City off the Northern Highway in the Belize District. It consists of some 18 square miles (47 square km) of basically subsistence farms.

Through a grassroots effort, villagers and landowners have committed to preserving the habitat necessary to insure a healthy population of black howler monkeys (known as baboons in Creole). With assistance from the WWF and the Zoological Society of Milwaukee County (United States), a small natural history museum and visitors' center has been built in Bermudian Landing, the most central location in the sanctuary.

FIVE BLUES LAKE NATIONAL PARK Established in 1992, the Five Blues Lake National Park is located in a beautiful and impressive setting in the forest-covered foothills of the Maya Mountains. It is a pristine tract of limestone terrain, honeycombed with unexplored cave systems and sinkholes—a karstic region—and teeming with spectacular wildlife.

The star attraction of the park is the lake. The lake is a cenote, a collapsed cave system also known as a blue hole. The lake showcases five unique shades of blue water, hence the name Five Blues Lake. It is thought that the lake was formed as the result of a blockage of an underground waterway, a common feature in karstic landscapes.

SAINT HERMAN'S BLUE HOLE NATIONAL PARK The Saint Herman's Blue Hole National Park (the inland Blue Hole) is located 12 miles (19 km) southeast of Belmopan on the Hummingbird Highway. The Blue Hole is a popular recreational spot, where water on its way from a tributary of the Sibun River emerges from a collapsed karst sinkhole.

The pool, from which the park takes its name, is a beautiful sapphire blue and attracts thousands of visitors in the summer months. After a short course through a natural jungle setting, the stream disappears into a large underwater cavern.

Two divers investigating this national monument, a former cave with enormous stalactites and stalagmites in the Blue Hole National Park in Belize.

BELIZEANS

A young woman from Belize City.

>**B**ELIZE HAS A VARIETY OF CULTURAL and linguistic traditions that came from migrant cultures. Through the years, these different cultures have been modified and localized by the immigrants or their descendants. Many Belizeans are of mixed racial ancestry.

The influx of Spanish-speaking people from other parts of Central America into Belize has been a cause of social tension, for until recently, Belize had been a mostly English-speaking Creole society. The constant migration of educated Creoles overseas has also aggravated the situation.

Belizean children giggling at the photographer.

CREOLES

Creolization in Belize is a complex synthesis of African and British heritages. The Creole people are descendants of African slaves brought to the Caribbean during the 18th and early 19th centuries and mixed with British settlers, as well as with subsequent African immigrants. The Creoles in Belize have styled their culture on British colonial examples. Most can speak formal English but use a Belizean Creole English at home and in informal situations. Until the early 1980s, Belizean Creoles made up close to 60 percent of the population of Belize, but today they are only about 25 percent. This is due to an influx of Spanish-speaking Central American refugees having come in from neighboring countries, as well as the emigration of about 85,000 Creoles abroad, primarily to the United States.

Creole kids testing the water by the beach.

African slaves in Belize were used mainly in logging, unlike those in other parts of the Caribbean who toiled on plantations. Some slaves did domestic work, while others farmed. Although the African slaves came from many different African ethnic groups, most of their cultures emphasized an important role for religion, and their religious leaders were influential people. Such leaders were also healers, judges, and teachers. Creoles now occupy a disproportionate number of government and police jobs, including the current prime minister, Dean Barrow. They also work in urban occupations on the waterfront and in service industries, and have established small farms and villages. They are largely concentrated in the coastal Belize District, in particular Belize City, which has about half of Belize's Creole community. Since independence, the Creoles have been the dominant culture in Belize, and tensions have arisen between them and the mestizos, who speak Spanish.

MESTIZOS

The mestizos, presently the largest population group in Belize, consists of 48 percent of the country's residents. There are two types of mestizo in the nation: those who are descendants of both Mexicans and Yucatec Mayans who fled from Yucatán in the mid 1800s, and those who migrated from Central America to Belize in the 1980s in search of refuge from violent civil wars in Petén, Guatemala.

The term "mestizo" refers generally to any person of mixed blood. In Central and South America, though, it refers more specifically to someone of combined Indian and European heritage. The Spanish-speaking mestizos first arrived in Belize by the thousands in the mid-19th century, following the outbreak of the Caste War in Yucatán between 1847 and 1853. Their numbers almost tripled the tiny population of Belize, which soared from 9,809 in 1845 to 25,635 in 1861.

These early mestizo immigrants tended to cluster in rural areas, particularly in northern and western Belize, and on cays such as Ambergris and Caulker. They are the backbone of agricultural production. Their numbers have grown vastly in the past 20 years from the influx of refugees from war-torn countries such as El Salvador, Nicaragua, and Guatemala. Tensions smolder now between the mestizos and the English-speaking Creoles over the identity of Belize—is it an English-speaking Caribbean country or a Spanish-speaking Central American nation?

THE MAYA

Mayas first came to Belize in A.D. 100, probably from the highlands of Guatemala and El Salvador. They consistently resisted British rule, and their numbers gradually dwindled; they were either chased out or were killed by European diseases or by the British. Modern Mayas are mainly immigrants from Guatemala and Mexico who fled their homes for a variety of reasons. There are three different groups of Mayas represented in modern Belize, each with its own language and cultural traditions.

The first group to arrive in Belize was the Yucatec Mayas who fled the Caste Wars in southern Mexico in the middle of the 19th century. They settled in northern Belize in the districts of Corozal and Orange Walk. The second group was the Mopan Mayas who lived in the Cayo and Toledo districts. They arrived from Guatemala in 1886, fleeing forced labor and taxation by Guatemalan authorities. The biggest Mopan settlement is San Antonio in Toledo. Mopans continue to practice subsistence agriculture, growing beans, corn, and root vegetables, but now are also producing honey, cacao, and rice for their cash economy.

A typical Mopan Mayan family.

The third group is the Kekchí Mayans who migrated to Belize from the Verapaz region of Guatemala to escape slavery at the hands of German coffee growers. They live in about 30 small communities in the Toledo District and are the poorest ethnic group in Belize. They practice an environmentally devastating slash-and-burn agriculture in which they cut down trees and burn them in order to clear the land. Like the Mopan, the Kekchí produce crops such as rice, citrus fruits, and cacao for sale in local markets.

A traditional Mayan skill is healing. Healers are knowledgeable about herbs and other plants that can cure or alleviate common ailments. That knowledge is now being used to develop herbal medicines and remedies for sale to Belizeans and abroad.

The total number of Belizean Mayan increased in the 20th century as a result of further emigration from Guatemala. Today, about 12 percent of the population of Belize is Mayan. At the peak of the vast Mayan Empire, archaeologists estimate that 1 to 2 million Mayans lived within the borders of Belize. Today, some Mayan groups, particularly those living in the more remote southern regions, are organizing themselves to protect their culture and way of life. This is part of a pan-Maya movement throughout Mexico and Central America. Considered inferior by the mestizos and Creoles alike, Mayans are counteracting this degrading conceit by pressurizing the government to establish a Maya Institute and a Maya Land Trust: an area of 500,000 acres (202,350 ha) dedicated to the Mayan people.

A group of Kekchí Mayans in Toledo District of Belize selling their handicrafts.

GARIFUNA

Garifuna, often called Black Caribs, are a mix of African, Arawak, and Carib ancestry. More precisely, the average Garifuna is 76 percent sub-Saharan African, 20 percent Arawak/Carib Indian, and 4 percent European. Their language is based on Carib, but most can speak either Standard English or Spanish in addition to their native tongue. Their music and dance, on the other hand, are chiefly African in origin. Traditionally fishermen, the Garifuna are settled mainly along the southern coast, at places such as Dangriga, Punta Gorda, and Barranco. Garifuna have also worked as farmers and laborers. They are famous for their linguistic abilities and are now widely employed in teaching and government jobs. Under the British, the Garifuna were treated as illegal squatters and prohibited from owning land. They were thought to be inferior and primitive, much as were the Mayans. In the past 20 years the Garifuna have been making efforts to celebrate and preserve their distinct culture and are hoping to introduce the Garifuna language to the national school system.

EAST INDIANS

East Indians have a long history in Belize, starting from the 1840s when tens of thousands of East Indians were contracted to work in the Caribbean British colonies. Many sugar plantations needed laborers at that time, so a system of indentured labor was introduced. Under this system, laborers were encouraged to come to the Caribbean from India to work for a "master" for a certain number of years, after which they were free to work as they pleased. Thousands of Indians agreed to come to the Caribbean, as they

Garifuna schoolgirls dressed up for a celebration.

The origin of the Garifuna, also known as Black Caribs, is a fascinating account. The Carib peoples were the indigenous groups that lived in the Caribbean and along the northern coast of the South American mainland. Farmers, hunters, and fishermen migrated to the Caribbean islands where they traded with the Arawaks, sometimes raiding their settlements and taking their women as wives. The resulting mixture of Carib and Arawak formed the Island Caribs. The Island Carib population had been depleted by hostile attacks from Europeans and imported disease by the start of the 16th century. Nevertheless, a large group of Caribs survived this genocide and continued to live on the island of Saint Vincent.

In 1635 two Spanish ships carrying African slaves shipwrecked near Saint Vincent. The Island Caribs sheltered the African survivors who intermarried with the Caribs, producing the Black Caribs. Throughout the 18th century, escaped slaves from all over the Caribbean added to their numbers, staunchly resisting European efforts to control and enslave them. Finally, in 1797 the British rounded up the Black Caribs and shipped them to Roatán, one of the islands off the coast of Honduras. From there, Black Caribs began to settle along the coast of Central America from modern day Bluefields in Nicaragua to Dangriga in Belize. On November 19, 1823, a large group of Black Caribs escaping the civil war in Honduras joined a small settlement at present-day Dangriga. This day is celebrated by Belizean Garifuna as Settlement Day.

Mennonite boys heading home with their water bottles in Lamanai, Orange Walk District.

were unemployed and often starving due to droughts at home. When their labor contracts were up, many stayed. Circumstances often forced these laborers to become "reindentured." Some went to the short-lived American settlement at Punta Gorda to work on the rice and sugar plantations, while others were signed on as sugar workers around Orange Walk, Corozal, and Toledo. East Indians have largely mixed with the Creoles, but their descendants can still be found at Calcutta in Corozal District and Forest Home in Toledo District.

MENNONITES

"The most striking features of the population of Belize are its quantity and its cultural diversity. . . . Belize is the least populous sovereign nation on the American mainland."—O. Nigel Bolland, *Belize: A New Nation in Central America*

Mennonites started arriving in Belize after 1958 when the Belizean government granted them exemption from military service and any compulsory insurance or welfare programs. Arriving from Mexico and Canada, they were granted permission by the government to establish colonies at Blue Creek, Shipyard, and Spanish Lookout.

Mennonites are Protestant Christians, related to the Anabaptists. Mennonites are named after Menno Simons, a Dutch priest who consolidated and institutionalized the work started by moderate Anabaptist leaders. They do not pay taxes, join armies, or send their children to state schools. Refraining from voting in national affairs, they also do not accept public office. In business affairs, however, they are skilled and active, mostly in the production and sale of poultry and dairy products, honey, and handmade furniture. Their communities practice a form of collective agriculture, speak a German dialect, and remain culturally apart from the rest of Belizean society, even though they succeed in local commerce.

ETHNIC GROUPS IN BELIZE

A Belizean government census taken in 2000 found the following breakdown by ethnic group:

Mestizo	*48.7 percent*
Creole	*24.9 percent*
Maya (Amerindian)	*10.6 percent*
Garifuna	*6.1 percent*
Others*	*9.7 percent*

*includes Asians, German Mennonites, and others of European descent.

"ANYTHING GOES"

Over the course of its history, Belize has become home to a wide range of people with distinct cultures and languages. There are numerous tensions and differences, although the prevailing attitude has been "anything goes," and there has been little direct racial or ethnic violence. At present none of the groups is in complete control of the future of the country. In fact, one of Belize's biggest challenges is to weave a national identity out of the many strands that will make up the Belizean tapestry.

To add to the cultural and linguistic potpourri of Belize, there are still white Creoles (descended from British settlers) and new white American immigrants living in Belize. Recent American arrivals have specialized in developing tourism, particularly in the cays, and are largely responsible for putting Belize on the travel map. In the late 1980s and 1990s the government also promoted immigration from Chinese areas such as Hong Kong and Taiwan. Visas to live and work in Belize, and even passports, have been sold for $25,000 to $35,000 per person, although there has been widespread criticism of this practice. These Asian migrants invest in Belize in order to gain Belizean citizenship or to be closer to the United States—the ultimate destination for many. Some, however, wish to make Belize their home and have built communities and schools in the Belize River Valley, while maintaining their native Chinese dialects.

The culture of British Honduras developed around groups that had fled persecution elsewhere— slaves, Mennonites, victims of the Caste Wars of Yucatán, and indigenous groups such as the Caribs and Maya." —Anne Sutherland, *The Making of Belize: Globalization on the Margins.*

FAMOUS BELIZEANS

Children learning about the conservation of wildlife at the Belize Zoo.

"LADY SMUGGLER" Although her real identity is unknown, this woman worked as a smuggler during the years of Prohibition in the United States. She was the captain of her own ship and made regular trips from Belize to Mexico with cargoes of rum for shipment to the United States. Her crew respected and obeyed her, and even Mexican officials were afraid of her. She was one of the many powerful Belizean women who played a part in their country's long and colorful history.

PETER WALLACE was a Scottish pirate. He was thought to be the first European to anchor his ships inside the barrier reef that runs along Belize's coast. Wallace built a temporary base camp at the mouth of the Belize River, where Belize City now stands, and enjoyed a lucrative career relieving the Spanish ships out of Panama of their precious cargoes.

MARCOS CANUL and other Mayans fled the civil war in Mexico in the 1850s to settle in northern Belize. They chose the land beyond the control of the logging companies and began to farm as they had done in Mexico. When the British tried to oust them, Canul led attacks on mahogany camps and settlements in the area. He was killed in the Mayan attack at Orange Walk in 1872. This attack by the Mayans was in retaliation for the constant sacking and burning of their villages by British woodcutters as they penetrated deeper into the interior for better stands of wood. Without Canul's brilliant leadership, the Mayan people would have been forced to give up their independence and live on reservations.

SHARON MATOLA is the founder of the Belize Zoo and Tropical Education Center, begun in 1983 to protect a collection of exotic animals that had been used in a documentary film. It is now home to more than 125 native

THE BELIZE ZOO

Started in 1983 by Sharon Matola, the Belize Zoo and Tropical Education Center was set up to provide a home for wild animals that had been used in the making of a documentary film. Today, the zoo makes a home to more than 125 native Belizean animals and sprawls across 29 acres (12 ha) of tropical savanna. These animals are orphans or born at the zoo or been rehabilitated or are gifts from other zoos. Welcoming more than 15,000 schoolchildren every

year, the zoo also organizes popular events such as April the Tapir's birthday party, summer camps, a science fair, and teacher-training and student career-training programs. It is also the headquarters for the Tapir Specialist Group and maintains an active captive breeding program for the green iguana.

Belizean species, and instructs people about wildlife and the ways to care for wildlife specimens. Matola, born in Baltimore, Maryland, was a former trainer of circus lions and also was an assistant to a nature filmmaker. When the filmmaker no longer needed his animal "stars," he told Matola to abandon the jaguars, peccaries, and other animals. Instead, Matola started an informal zoo and spent thousands of hours trying to raise money to feed and house the homeless animals. More than a random collection of cages, her zoo is educational and, together with her children's books about nature, has changed the attitude of Belizean children toward their environment. Sharon Matola is also an active campaigner for the rights and protection of native Belizean animals and their natural habitats from the disruptive influences of land development and urbanization. She received a Whitley Award in 1998 for her work in protecting the scarlet macaw of Belize. Matola spearheaded a field research program and a complementary education program to save this bird, one of the prime victims of the illegal pet trade.

LIFESTYLE

A boy gets his hair cut at the barber's on Ambergris Caye.

A S WITH ALL THINGS BELIZEAN, there is a lot of diversity packed into a very small space. There is an endless procession of lifestyles, whether urban or rural; mainland or islander; rich or poor; male or female; Creole, Mayan, Garifuna, mestizo, Indian, or Mennonite.

ISLANDERS

Islanders living on the cays have withstood dramatic changes to their way of life in the past 20 years. Such heavily populated cays as Ambergris

Many local girls in Belize join clubs such as this Girl Guide group.

For many ethnic groups and for the lower social and economic groups in Belize, a formal marriage ceremony is unnecessary. However, family ties beyond the immediate family are strong, including close links to grandparents, aunts and uncles, and nephews and nieces. Marriage between members of different groups has also been very common.

73

The swimming pool at a resort in San Pedro. Thatched cabana cottages provide tropical housing and is a hit with many tourists.

and Caulker have become tourist meccas since the 1980s. Previously, people on the islands depended on fishing to make a living and were isolated from the mainland. They traded with Belize City to obtain lumber for house construction and food that they could not grow themselves, but island life was fairly removed from the hustle and bustle of the city. Cay dwellers depended on each other, and there was almost no crime, for everyone knew everyone else.

The influx of tourists, however, has imposed many changes upon this tranquil existence. Such changes have been more dramatic in San Pedro, on Ambergris Caye, than on Caye Caulker, but there are many similarities. Land values, for example, have increased tremendously, and in some areas resident Belizeans have been priced out of the market as Americans and other foreigners compete to buy beachfront property. The relatively recent availability of regular transportation to the mainland means that local residents can reach services in Belize City easily, but it also means that people come and go at such a rate that life has become more impersonal, and crime often goes unpunished. Crime has partly arrived with tourism because tourists bring behavior such as drug use with them and often travel with expensive belongings that are a source of temptation to poor islanders. Some islanders have traded their fishing nets for a tourist business such as a small hotel, restaurant, or guide service. One social change from tourism is that women can earn their own money and gain some independence. Belizean islanders continue to adapt to ever changing economic and social circumstances.

FAMILIES AND CHILDREN

The family is very important to Belizeans of all backgrounds. Wherein the colonial and independent governments have been unwilling or unable to provide basic services for the population, people have relied on their close and extended families for work, child care, health care, social assistance, and companionship. The form that the family takes differs from one community to another, but the overriding aura of family and kinship is universal.

Creole Belizeans tend to have matriarchal households. This pattern is found across the Caribbean and stems from a history of slavery. In early colonial times male slaves often worked far from Belize City, cutting lumber, while women worked as domestic help in the city. In modern times migration for work opportunities has continued, with men emigrating to the United States. For Belizean men who cannot afford to provide regular family support or to pay for a church wedding ceremony, there are common-law marriages and "visiting" arrangements. A common-law marriage is one where the couple is not legally married but live together in a stable relationship. "Visiting" relationships are when the father of the children lives with his own mother and siblings and only visits the mother of his children occasionally. He will contribute to that household when he has work. Creole women become the backbone of the family, as it is they who provide for children and help each

With the men often being at work away from home, it is usually the women who look after the daily needs of their families.

A traditional Mennonite family in Belize.

other with child care. Often children are raised by a grandmother if their mother is a single parent and has to work, or emigrates to the United States to seek work.

For wealthier Belizeans, the norm is a nuclear or extended family. This means that husband and wife live with their children and sometimes with their parents or siblings, too. Everyone contributes to the family unit. In rural communities women help with agricultural work and maintain the house, while men farm and sometimes work for wages. Older relatives provide child care when necessary. Beyond the household is a wider network of relatives who can be relied on in times of need.

Family size differs across the cultural spectrum with recent mestizo immigrants tending to have more children (three to four on average per couple). In matriarchal households the children born to one woman may not necessarily share one father. These children used to be discriminated against by the community and viewed under the law as illegitimate. Under colonial law, children born to parents who were not legally married were considered to have no rights to paternal support or to any part of their father's estate. Since many Belizeans are born to unwed parents, this posed a serious problem. In 1980 the law was changed to enforce child support by the father. Children born out of wedlock are now considered to have the same rights to their parents' estates as legitimate children.

LEAVING BELIZE

The first wave of Belizean emigrants to the United States arrived as agricultural workers during the labor shortage of World War II. A small trickle of 2,000 turned into a flood in subsequent years. Official numbers recorded 55,000 to 60,000 Belizeans in the United States, concentrated in cities such as New York, Los Angeles, Houston, Chicago, New Orleans, and Miami. Though these are the official numbers, there are probably at least another 100,000 Belizeans living illegally in the United States. Between 1980 and 1991, 41,000 legal immigrants entered the United States from Belize. The bulk of the emigrants (75 percent) are from the Creole and Garifuna segments of the population. Creoles have an advantage because they speak English, and the entrepreneurial Garifuna learn English quickly and effectively. Since their initial entry as agricultural workers, Belizeans have turned away from rural work and moved mostly to cities in search of industrial and service sector jobs. Given the high unemployment and limited opportunities at home, young Belizeans aspire to something better abroad.

A shopping trip for this city mom and her children starts their busy day.

This drain of people from the already minuscule population of Belize has had a number of effects on those left behind. Until recently, most Belizean emigrants to the United States were the better-educated middle classes from Belize City and Dangriga. This has created a "brain drain," as the more promising young workers fail to return once they complete their education abroad. Immigrants in the United States, on the other hand, are often a source of income for their families in Belize. Their remittances account for some 12 to 15 percent of the Belizean gross domestic product, up to 10 percent of its per capita income, and are a significant part of household budgets—and the economy. This has created a dual currency system in which people use both the Belizean and the U.S. dollar in their daily transactions, adding a dimension to consumer spending in Belize. Only a small percentage of remittances are sent through official channels; most arrive in the form of cash gifts.

The departure of English-speaking Creoles, together with the recent influx of Spanish-speaking mestizos from other parts of Central America, is changing the cultural and social balance of the country. New mestizo arrivals overwhelmingly are poor, uneducated, rural people who choose to live in the countryside in communities with other mestizos. Spanish has become the majority language, and these new immigrants will soon form a sizeable voting bloc. Remaining Creoles worry that this Spanish-speaking mass will threaten their dominant position in politics. The government has vacillated between welcoming new people to Belize to make up for large labor losses, particularly in export agriculture (sugar, citrus fruits, and bananas), and restricting their entry because they are largely Spanish-speaking and poor.

The economic crisis of the 1990s affected the outward flow of Belizeans. Fewer Belizeans went as legal immigrants to the United States (60 percent entered or stayed in the United States illegally). Even fewer have maintained ties with their families at home, being younger and less well educated and having to cope with the stress of living costs in the United States. Those who do return take back American cultural influences. Sadly, some who have been deported from the United States because of illegal activities have also taken back violent behavior and drug use. Many returnees, however, are contributing wholesomely to the development of Belize.

Because of its high emigration rate, Belize encourages immigration. In 2000 the net emigration rate was -2.3 migrants per 1,000 population. Worker remittances in 2000 amounted to $22 million. The population of Belize increased significantly in 1993, with 40,000 Central American refugees and other immigrants, mostly from Guatemala and El Salvador. This offset the heavy Creole departures to North America. The negotiations of the United Nations High Commissioner for Refugees (UNHCR) with the government produced two significant developments in 1999. First, as of February 1999 refugees are able to apply for naturalization after 5 years of residence in the country. Second, in May 1999 the government enacted an amnesty program, offering permanent resident status for illegal immigrants and unregistered refugees. By June 30, 1999, some 10,000 families had registered. The total number of individual immigrants in Belize in 2000 was 17,000.

RURAL VERSUS URBAN LIVING

Like most developing countries, Belize has experienced a drift toward urbanization. By 1970, 54 percent of Belizeans lived in urban centers. Since then, this trend has reversed; in 2003, 48 percent lived in rural areas and 52 percent in cities. This pattern is not the same for all districts. Belize District, in particular, is very urbanized, with a fairly constant 79.5 percent of its population living in Belize City. The other districts, Cayo, Toledo, Stann Creek, Orange Walk, and Corozal, have always been more rural than urban. The trend toward urbanization slowed and then reversed through the 1970s and 1980s because of migration patterns. The thousands of Belizeans who left the country mostly came from urban areas; this exodus was offset by the 40,000 mestizo newcomers who arrived after 1980 and settled in rural locales.

Rural dwellers in Belize do not have equal access to essential services such as health care and schools and are much poorer than urban dwellers. On the other hand, urban dwellers face higher crime rates and poor sanitation. A person's class also fixes the quality of his or her urban life.

A social security program was created in the 1980s to provide pensions for senior citizens and to extend assistance to sick, disabled, pregnant, and unemployed workers and the families of deceased insured workers.

Simple rural homes dot the verdant countryside near the village of San Antonio.

EDUCATION

The literacy rate in Belize is 76.9 percent, which is high compared with other Central American countries. The existing educational system is badly in need of reform and expansion, however, to handle the growing numbers of Spanish-speaking, poor, and rural students. Prime Minister Dean Barrow has committed 25 percent of his budget to confront some of these increasing pressures.

The Belizean educational system is based on British education and is broken into three levels: primary, secondary, and tertiary. Belizean children begin their eight years of primary education with two years of "infant" classes, followed by six "standards." Secondary education is divided into four "forms." This is folowed by a two-year post-secondary course to prepare students for the Cambridge Advanced or "A-level" examinations.

A teacher discusses the solution to a problem with her class.

As recently as 1980, the majority of secondary schools were under religious management. By the latter half of the 1980s, while religious groups controlled the majority of primary schools, the government or private, community-based boards of governors administered more than half of the nation's secondary institutions. The government's involvement at the secondary level is relatively a new development.

Education in Belize is compulsory between the ages of 6 and 14 years for primary education. Primary education is free, but related expenses, such as uniforms and books, are a financial strain on poor families. Secondary schools and apprenticeship and vocational programs can accommodate only half of the children who complete their primary schooling.

The government of the previous prime minister, Said Musa, had drafted "The New Education Charter" to address some of these problems. The charter included plans to build 1,000 new schoolrooms, train more teachers, establish a school cafeteria program for poor children, set up a subsidized textbook program, and introduce an improved curriculum for elementary schools. As of 2010, there are 1,220 students on scholarships at the University of Belize and an additional 2,914 are presently receiving financial grants.

Classes are sometimes held outside the classroom so students can get a breath of fresh air.

Twelve percent of children ages 6 to 14 years are working and do not attend school.

The Stann Creek Medical Centre in Dandriga is typical of the many medical facilities found throughout Belize.

HEALTH

Belize fares better than some of its neighbors, such as Honduras, in health care, but it still faces some serious health problems. With mosquito eradication programs functioning in Belize, malaria is far less of a problem now than it was as recently as the 1980s. Yet there are several thousand new cases of malaria reported in Belize every year, mainly in the south and in remote areas of the north and west. Occurrences of malaria are rare in populated areas such as Belize City and on the cays. Dengue fever, another mosquito-borne disease, is another grave health issue. There was a dengue fever outbreak in 2009. Controlling malaria and dengue involves general hygiene in the form of managed garbage disposal as well as area programs using insecticides. Many Belizeans have died of AIDS (acquired immune deficiency syndrome) since the 1980s. Belize, happily, has managed to bring its AIDS epidemic under control, and the prevalence rate of HIV (the virus that can bring on AIDS) is now 2.1 percent. Belizeans, especially babies and children, are also vulnerable to diarrhea caused by unclean water and inadequate or absent sanitation systems.

A grim estimate holds that 18 percent of Belize's rural population does not have access to clean water.

The majority of Belizeans have access to government hospitals, clinics, maternal and child care, and dental facilities. Infant mortality rates have been reduced by improved water supplies, disease control, waste disposal systems, and vaccination programs. Major medical advances in Belize have been accomplished over the years—there are now two private hospitals and the national government runs public hospitals in all major towns. Medical doctors in Belize are trained predominantly in neighboring Guatemala, Mexico, Cuba, and Jamaica.

HOUSING

There are a few main styles of house construction in Belize. One is the wooden clapboard style that is found all throughout the English-speaking Caribbean. These buildings can be seen along the coast and on the cays. Smaller houses may have only one or two indoor rooms with most cooking taking place outdoors. Larger wooden houses often have a covered veranda encircling the front and sides where people can relax and enjoy the sea breezes. Such houses usually do not have glass windows unless the owners are wealthy. Instead there are hinged slotted shutters that can be closed against rain but still allow air circulation. In low-lying areas like Belize City, houses are often built on stilts so that they remain dry during the rainy season. In rural inland areas whitewashed mud or wood houses and thatch houses are more commonly found. Across the country, there is a trend toward using concrete blocks and metal roofs as substitutes for more traditional materials. Concrete needs less upkeep than wood, which is susceptible to termites and decay, or than wattle-and-daub houses that erode in the rain.

A typical wood frame house on stilts in Caye Caulker.

Belize City has a great number of old, run-down wooden houses that are riddled with destructive termites and wood lice. Many of these houses stand on shaky wooden posts. On the outskirts of the city there are numerous shacks thrown together by poor squatters. In the inland and rural areas many villages have inadequate housing and supporting infrastructure, especially sanitation. There is a large population of immigrants from surrounding Central American countries congregated on the outskirts of larger towns, dwelling in temporary, substandard housing. The government has pledged to build 10,000 new houses over a five-year period.

RELIGION

Parishioners during a mass at Corozal's Saint Francis Xavier Roman Catholic Church.

FOREIGN CATHOLICS FREQUENTLY visit the country for special gospel revivals. The Greek Orthodox Church has a presence in Santa Elena. Jehovah's Witnesses have experienced a significant increase in membership in recent years.

According to the Witnesses, around 3 percent of the population attended at least one of their religious meetings in 2007. The Church of Jesus Christ of Latter-day Saints (Mormons) claims 3,300 followers in the country. There are a few other religions and belief systems as well, including Islam, Hinduism, Judaism, and the Baha'i faith. As in everything else, Belize's religions are a liberal mixture of traditions and people.

A decorated facade adorns a small Christian church in Belize City.

Religious freedom is guaranteed in Belize. Nearly 80 percent of Belizeans are Christian, with 49.6 percent of them being Roman Catholic and 29 percent Protestant.

CHRISTIANITY

The original Baymen were all Protestants, so the first church to be established in the new territory was the Anglican Church of England, which was incorporated into the Jamaican diocese in 1824. At that time, Christianity and church attendance was exclusively a white phenomenon. Back home in England, humanitarian church reformers were pressuring the Colonial Office to adopt policies to protect slaves in British colonies from mistreatment. The reformers also conducted missionary work among the slaves in efforts to teach them English and introduce them to Christianity. But the Church of England prohibited its missionaries from acting against the wishes of the slave owners, and this constraint prompted an antiestablishment evangelical movement among Anglicans and the rise of nonconformist churches such as the Baptist Church and Wesleyan Methodist Church. Both of the young churches set up missions in Belize in the 1820s. They gave the slaves basic education and helped them through the transition from bondage to freedom in 1838 when slavery was abolished in all British dominions. These two reform churches still operate in Belize today.

A Garifuna congregation attending mass at a Roman Catholic church in Dangriga.

Present-day Belize is largely Roman Catholic. When the Yucatec and Mopan Mayans came from Mexico, and when the Kekchí came from Guatemala, they brought Roman Catholicism with them. The vast numbers of Central American economic and political refugees that have made their ways to Belize in the past 20 years have been Roman Catholics. Many Garifuna are also Roman Catholic. The Catholic Church first arrived in the persons of two Jesuit priests in 1851, and the first church was built in Corozal Town. In 1883 the Sisters of Mercy arrived to found a girls' school, Saint Catherine's Academy, and a convent. Jesuits founded the prestigious Saint John's College in 1887. Traditionally a private school for upper class boys, graduation from this school certified that a youth was of the right background and ability to be a leader in business or politics. In modern Belize, Saint John's College still offers a top quality education but has opened its doors to the wider population, including young women, through a system of scholarships. It is also innovative in the arts and literature. Saint John's College today counts more than 1,500 students in its student body.

Other churches were established during colonial times, including a Scottish Presbyterian Church in 1851 and the American-based Seventh-day Adventists, which started a Belizean mission in 1891. The Seventh-day Adventist Church has 34,000 adherents worshiping in 76 churches and congregations in Belize. Evangelical Christian churches from the United States have gained support in Belize. They began sending missions to Belize and other parts of Central and South America in the 1970s and 1980s. For a while in the early 1980s, evangelical Bible study groups, storefront churches, social programs, and schools sprang up all over the country. The arrival of television, however, has noticeably slowed down this growth in urban areas. In remote rural areas, especially the Mayan south, missionaries have been more successful in converting people, and there has been an increase in the number of church schools and a welcome decline in alcohol abuse.

Dating back to 1847, Saint John's Cathedral in Belize City is the oldest Anglican parish in Central America. The church was rebuilt after being completely destroyed by a hurricane in 1931.

The Mennonite religion is a type of Protestant Christianity. Mennonites believe in following the New Testament of the Christian Bible, particularly the Sermon on the Mount. They believe that there should be a strict separation of church and state. So, for example, they refuse to have their children educated in state-run schools

and prefer to operate their own schools in the German language. As part of their commitment to the "simple life" promoted in the Bible, they reject fancy clothes and the use of machines. They believe in the supremacy and singularity of God and do not worship false idols. This means that they do not support such symbols as a national flag or anthem and do not hold public office. They are pacifists, which means that they reject any and all forms of violence and will not bear arms or go to war for their country.

Separated as they are from national life, all these beliefs and practices have made it difficult for Mennonites to live in peace. Mennonite communities in their Swiss homeland were often persecuted by other religions and the state, so in the 17th century many of them settled in other places, arriving, for example, in Pennsylvania in 1683, where they formed a group eventually called the Pennsylvania Dutch (from Deutsch, spoken German). There was also a large exodus of Mennonites from Europe to Canada and Mexico following World War I. Then, in the 1950s, fearing that the government was going to try to force them to join the social security system, many Mexican Mennonites left Mexico to settle in Belize. They signed a special agreement with the Belize government that exempted them from military service and certain forms of taxation, while concomitantly guaranteeing them complete freedom to practice their own distinctive form of Protestantism and to farm within their closed communities. They also freely practice their own form of local government and run their own schools, banks, and businesses.

The Mennonites originally established communities in large uninhabited tracts of land in the districts of Corozal, Orange Walk, and Cayo. Widely respected throughout the countryside for their scrupulous work ethic, the Mennonites have turned sections of rural Belize into neat, highly productive farmland and spotless dairies. After building a road from the Blue Creek settlement to Orange Walk, the Mennonites later founded Spanish Lookout and Shipyard. Although isolating themselves from the other cultures of Belize, they provide indispensable services and products to the entire economy, in which they participate fully, mostly in the production and sale of poultry and dairy products. In addition, Mennonites craft a variety of elegant, sturdy wooden furniture sold everywhere in the country.

RASTAFARIANISM

Rastafarians worship Haile Selassie I, former emperor of Ethiopia. His precoronation name was Ras (prince) Tafari. Rastafarians consider him a divine being, the Messiah, and the champion of the black race. A core belief of Rastafarianism is that black people are a reincarnation of the ancient Israelites and will one day return to Africa to establish a Black Zion under the leadership of a black king.

Rastafarianism is a political-religious movement with its center in the highlands of Jamaica. Most Rastas outside Jamaica practice only a few of the principles of the religion. In Belize it is mostly young Creole men who are attracted to the Rasta look and lifestyle. They are often unemployed and depend on tourists to support them. Dogmatic Rastas abstain from liquor and red meat but believe that marijuana has spiritual properties. The Rastas have traditionally been involved with the use of marijuana as part of their religion, so it followed that they became involved with the cultivation and marketing of the plant. They are easily recognized as they do not cut their hair but style it into braids called dreadlocks. The religion is associated with popular reggae singer Bob Marley.

A Rastafarian teen in Dangriga.

The *dugu* ritual has recently become more common. In the 1850s and 1860s the *dugu* was rarely practiced because of fear that the government (appointed by the British) would ban the rites altogether. Now, however, the *dugu* is practiced in many countries throughout Central America, but mainly in Belize.

GARIFUNA BELIEFS

Although the Garifuna attend Roman Catholic and Methodist churches, they also maintain ancient beliefs and rituals, at times combining them with the formal practice of Catholicism. There are three main ancestral rites practiced by the Garifuna: the *amuyadahani* (bathing the spirit of the dead); the *chugu* (feeding the dead); and the *dugu* (feasting of the dead). *Dugu* (DOO-goo) is the most sacred, elaborate, and best demonstration of Garifuna respect, appreciation, and communion with their ancestors.

Dugu rites are performed at the request of a deceased ancestor, which is made known in a ceremony called *arairaguni* (bringing down) held by a *buyae*, or medium. The *buyae* calls upon his *hiuruha* or spirit helper to explain a particular problem, such as an unexplained death in the family. The *buyae* and *hiuruha* communicate with the family's deceased ancestors, or *gubida*, to ascertain the cause of this death, which may be a form of punishment by an angered great-grandfather. The *gubida* will then request a *dugu* as an appeasement. Preparations for this rite involve inviting relatives and friends from Belize and abroad, obtaining particular foods and beverages requested by that ancestor, and setting a date for the rite with the *buyae*, who will also inform other official performers, including drummers, performers dressed in red, singers, and selected fishermen. There are four types of dance during the *dugu*: a semisacred song of the women, a song and dance of supplication, a dance of rejoicing, and a dance in circular formation. The participants may go into a trance and assume the characteristics of the *gubida* during the ceremony.

FOLK BELIEFS AND LEGENDS

Belizean traditional beliefs came from African influences in Creole and Garifuna cultures, and from Mayan influence through mestizo customs. Some of their views are found in other parts of Central America and the Caribbean. Some of what Westerners call superstitions include the belief that seeing a certain species of black butterfly will cause an early death or bad luck, or that shoes should be crossed at night so that evil spirits will not occupy them, bringing misfortune to the owner the next day. From Mayan tradition comes the belief that dreams are omens of the future. For example, a dream with red tomatoes in it means a baby will die.

In addition to folk beliefs, legends are popular among Belizeans. Local children learn about Belizean dwarfs, known by their Spanish name, *duendes* (doo-EN-days). *Duendes* are evil but possess magical powers. If they capture you, they can make you go crazy, but they can also turn you into an expert musician on the instrument of your choice. They are said to live in the forest, and if you see them, you should salute, being careful to hide your thumb as they do not have thumbs and are jealous of those who do have. They are said to be short and covered in thick dark hair. Some commentators claim that the ancient Maya portrayed *duendes* in their carvings.

Another forest dweller is the *sisimito* (see-see-MEE-toh), a hairy, manlike beast similar to the yeti of Asia and Sasquatch of North America. *Sisimitos* have a reputation for killing men and stealing their women for mates. For a man to look into the *sisimito's* eyes foretells his death within a month. The *sisimito* wants desperately to learn how to make fire and to talk, and so they may abduct children to teach them language or sit enraptured for hours around an abandoned campfire watching the coals. *Sisimitos* in Latin American societies have been reported for hundreds of years.

Another folktale features a mysterious, ghostly pirate ship called the *Jack O'Lantern* that people claimed to have seen in the Stann Creek area. The vessel is lit with flickering lanterns that are blamed for luring fishermen onto the coastal reef to their deaths.

The Deer Dance traces its origins to traditional Mayan folklore. Maya dancers dressed as hunters, sacred deer, and a jaguar perform this annual dance where the trickster jaguar antagonizes the hapless hunters.

LANGUAGE

Schoolboys in San Ignacio showing tourist literature.

ONE OF THE PRIMARY WAYS THAT cultural difference is expressed in Belize is through language. Standard English is the official language of the nation, but the majority of Belizeans speak localized versions of English or other languages at home and on the street.

Young friends chatting on their car in **Belize City**.

Belizean Creole
English is very
close to Nicaraguan
Creole English.

CREOLE ENGLISH

As a former colony of Great Britain, Belize retains Standard English as its official language. This is the language of instruction in government schools and for formal diplomatic and governmental business. Nevertheless, it is not the most widely spoken form of English. Creole English, a blend of different influences, including Spanish and African languages, is the lingua franca of the country. To speakers of Standard English, whether British or American, Creole English is only partly understandable. Today, Belizean Creole is the native language of the majority of the country's inhabitants. Many of them speak Standard English as well, and a rapid process of decreolization is going on. Some words are the same, but pronunciation and intonation are quite different. Belizean Creole English shares many things in common with the Creole English of Jamaica, another former British colony. Since the beginning of the tourism boom in Belize, Americans and Canadians are also adding their style of English to the melting pot. With the arrival of television in the early 1980s, there has been an even greater American cultural influence.

A colorful sign in Caye Caulker urges the public not to litter because many go barefoot in the area.

Creole English is quite similar to Standard English but is spoken with a different cadence, and some words are different. Here are some examples of proverbs in Creole and Standard English:

Creole English:

"Punkin never bear watermelon."

"Coward man keep sound bone."

"Fool dey talk, but dey no fool—dey lisson."

Standard English:

"Pumpkin plants don't produce watermelons."

"A coward doesn't get injured."

"Fools talk a lot but wise people listen."

BELIZEAN SPANISH

Just as there are varieties of English spoken in Belize, there are also different types of Spanish spoken by Belizeans of different origins. The first mestizos who came from Mexico and Guatemala in the 19th century now speak what they call "kitchen Spanish," thus named to reflect its degraded form. These Spanish speakers have been exposed to English, as spoken by the British and Creoles, for so long that many English and Creole expressions and words have entered their Spanish. Some examples of Standard English words typically found in this type of Belizean Spanish are shop, lunch, tip (as in a gratuity), mile, holiday, creek, and pool. Johnnycake (a type of flatbread or pancake), bra-in-law (brother-in-law), and John Canoe (a Garifuna dance) are from Creole English. In addition to English words, there are also changes

An English-Spanish sign in Belize.

in Spanish grammar in which the gender of a noun is switched or a verb is used differently. New strains of Spanish have entered the Belizean linguistic soup with recent immigrants from Guatemala, El Salvador, and Nicaragua. Their Spanish is less influenced by English expressions because the speakers come from monolingual Spanish countries.

OTHER LANGUAGES

English and Spanish are the dominant languages, but other languages are also spoken in Belize. Garifuna is the mother tongue of about 7 percent of the population. This language combines features of Arawak and Carib with African languages. Garifuna is spoken in homes and areas like Dangriga where the majority of the population is Garifuna. In other parts of the country, Garifunas speak either Creole English or Spanish. About 10 percent of Mayan people have retained their languages. The Kekchí Mayans of Toledo still learn Kekchí as their first language, although most are bilingual in Spanish. Northern Mayans tend to speak Spanish as their mother tongue and have lost their Mayan language completely.

Finally, the Belizean Mennonites speak the Plautdietsch German dialect and teach their own children in this language. This German is quite distinct from modern European German. Its roots are from the Low German spoken about a century ago, which had Prussian and Dutch influences, when the ancestors of this religious group left Europe. Most Mennonite men, and some of the women, also speak English and Spanish to communicate with their non-German-speaking neighbors.

In 2001, the United Nations Educational, Scientific, and Cultural Organization (UNESCO) declared the Garifuna language, dance, and music to be a "Masterpiece of the Oral and Intangible Heritage of Humanity."

LINGUISTIC CHANGES

Apart from languages changing internally, there have also been significant adaptations in the overall linguistic landscape of Belize. Around 1950, 60 percent of Belizeans spoke English as their first language, 22 percent spoke Spanish, 10 percent spoke a Mayan dialect, and the remainder spoke Garifuna or another language. By 1980 English speakers dropped to 51 percent and Spanish speakers increased to 32 percent, although Mayan speakers held constant at 10 percent. Today, English speakers remain predominant as English is the only official language of Belize and is the main language used in government and education. Although only a small percentage of the population speaks it as their main language at home, 54 percent can speak it very well, and another 26 percent can speak some English. Creole is considered to be their primary language by 32.9 percent of Belizeans. It is also a second or third language for another 40 percent of the multilingual country. Because it is English-based, all Creole speakers can understand English.

A Garifuna boy in Hopkins Village proudly shows his English workbook.

Spanish has been spoken in Belize since the 1840s, when mestizo refugees first came to Belize. Today it is commonly spoken at home by 46 percent of the population (mostly mestizos), and most other people are able to communicate in this language, too. Mayan languages, Garifuna, and the German dialect, Plautdietsch, are spoken by about 15.6 percent of the population. This shift, due in a large part to migration, has resulted in the emergence of a new linguistic populace in which bilingualism in Spanish and English is increasingly necessary.

VERBAL SKILLS

Many writers on Belize comment on the importance of verbal interaction in daily life. This is not surprising when one considers the history of telecommunications in this little country. In the early 1970s the telephone system connected only 3,800 homes and businesses. Caye Caulker had one telephone for the whole island in 1982. With satellite and cellular technology, most middle-class Belizeans now own telephones. There were 31,100 telephone lines in Belize as of 2008. Previously, most interaction between individuals took place in face-to-face meetings. That meant that one's word was one's honor, and a verbal agreement was enough to seal a deal. Hence, linguistic skills were highly prized and cultivated. Telling a good story was a way to amuse and impress friends, even if the facts were stretched a little for

Village neighbors relaxing and exchanging stories at a corner market in San Pedro, Ambergris Cay.

THE EARLY DAYS OF THE TELEPHONE

Author Anne Sutherland has lived in Belize for more than 30 years. In her book The Making of Belize, *she recounts a story of how Belizeans used telephones when they first came to Caye Caulker:*

"Communication was strictly face-to-face. This may be why in Belize, when the telephone came in, it was common to have the following phone conversation:

> *(Ring)* Hello.
> Is Lindsay there?
> Yes. *(Click)*
> *(Ring)* Hello.
> Hello, I asked if Lindsay was there.
> Yes, I told you he is.
> Well, may I speak with him?
> Oh, sure. Why didn't you say so?

"People assumed that the purpose of a phone call was to find out if someone else was there so the caller could come over and talk face-to-face. No one could expect to get anything done by speaking on the telephone."

entertainment value. Creole English is known for the colorful way that ideas are expressed and is considered to be superior to Standard English in this regard. With the arrival of modern telecommunications, including television, video, DVD, and cell phones, face-to-face conversation and storytelling have given way to long-distance communication. Belizeans now are entertained by satellite programs and foreign movies.

ARTS

A Mayan handweaver selling clothing
at a beach on Caye Caulker.

WHILE BELIZE HAS HAD TO struggle to produce its own artistic, literary, and musical traditions against the overwhelming influence of the British and now faces the invasive challenge of American culture, there is ample evidence that Belizeans are creative and resilient enough to overcome the odds despite being a small country with limited resources.

Local handicrafts such as straw baskets and artistic carvings on wood, slate, and stone can be found at the National Handicrafts Center in Belize. Belizean arts and crafts reflect the whole spectrum of cultural diversity in Belize.

The brightly decorated Toucan Too Gift Shop in San Pedro attracts tourists.

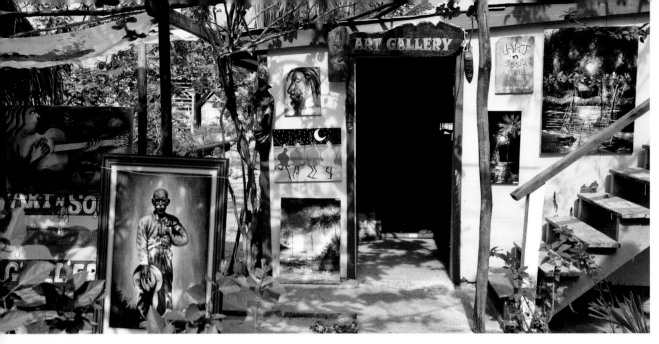

A local art gallery in Placencia.

CULTURAL INFLUENCES

Being part Central American and part Caribbean, Belize enjoys cultural influences from many sources. It is also a country in transition, so cultural traditions that once dominated the arts are now sharing space with new ideas. European influences are felt most strongly in language, where English and Spanish dominate. Indigenous cultural traditions are apparent in the language and practices of the Kekchí, Yucatec, and Mopan Mayans, as well as in the language of the Garifuna. African traditions, particularly in music, reach into both Creole and Garifuna rhythms and instruments. In the past 20 years the newest influence has been a global one—the cultural exports of the United States. This cultural phenomenon affects, in differing degrees, every country and culture on the planet, but Belize is particularly susceptible because of its intimate social ties with the United States through the emigration of so many of its people. Top 40 music hits are frequently heard on Belizean radio, and clothing styles, particularly in urban centers, are influenced by American television and movies. Tourists, who are bearers of culture, also bring their habits and customs with them. While this makes it extremely difficult to keep venerable local traditions alive, American tourists are providing a small market for some Belizean artists and craftspeople who otherwise would not be able to make a living from their work.

Painter, author, and entertainer Angela Gegg, who works under the name Proshka, is one of Belize's hottest female artists. She has been featured in more than 20 solo and joint art shows.

LITERARY ARTS

Under the British, Belizean literature was written exclusively in Standard English. Now there is a growing movement to write in Creole English, the lingua franca of most Belizeans. There has been a growing nationalism and pride in Creole culture and an eagerness to draw on African and European elements of Belizean heritage.

The first Belizean novelist to gain recognition was Zee Edgell. Her first book, *Beka Lamb*, was published in 1982. She advanced her critical success with three more novels: *In Times Like These* (1991), *The Festival of San Joaquin* (1997), and *Time and the River* (2007). Women are central characters in all four of her novels, which are set in Belize and grapple with problems the country faced during and after colonialism. *The Festival of San Joaquin* deals with environmental profiteering and the role of evangelical churches in modern Belize. *Beka Lamb* portrays a young Creole girl in Belize City in the 1950s and celebrates Belizean life by its unapologetic focus on everyday aspects of local family life, education, and the politics of the early independence movement.

Since the end of colonialism, new magazines and journals have sprung up, primarily in Belize City. Cubola is a local publishing house that specializes in young Belizean writers of fiction and nonfiction. *Belizean Studies* is a journal published by the Belizean Studies Association of Saint John's College that provides an outlet for Belizean research and writing. In November 2010 *Belizean Studies* became 32 years old. *Amandala*, the most politically independent newspaper in Belize, provides Belizeans a forum for political discussion.

This Mayan-inspired carved sign in Stann Creek contains old Mayan symbols.

VISUAL ARTS

The art scene has flourished in Belize ever since the rise of the independence movement of the 1950s and 1960s. In its early stages, Belizean artists and craftspeople were scattered and disorganized, and there were no formal means by which the government or schools could support the development of young artists. Some pioneers, such as Philip Lewis, formed the group Soul to Art in 1974 to promote painters and sculptors through organized exhibits; more than 50 shows were held in Belize and Jamaica. More recently, Saint John's College has started offering an arts program that is already bearing fruit. Before this program, aspiring artists either had to teach themselves or leave the country for formal training. Unfortunately, as also with medical doctors, many who are educated abroad choose not to return. Nevertheless, the relaxed pace of life and the opportunity to sell their works to tourists make Belize a new artists' haven.

Paintings and handcarved items by local Belizean artists are sold in San Pedro on Ambergris Caye.

MUSIC

Belize shares many of its musical styles with Central America and the English-speaking Caribbean. A significant exception to this is a style called punta rock that originated among Belizean Garifuna people. Punta rock is based on traditional Garifuna dance and song patterns. The punta dance was often performed at wakes. The music is provided by drummers and by

The Original Turtle Shell Band, a group of Garifuna musicians, performing punta rock on a beach in Dangriga.

spectators clapping their hands and chanting. A couple moves around the dance floor using quick sideways shuffling steps and hip movements. Women can also dance the punta alone. The dance is accompanied by a type of call-and-response song in which local characters are derided or criticized without being named. In the early 1990s a modern form of punta developed among pop bands, and became quite popular in Belize and Honduras. The new punta combined Garifuna rhythms and song styles with calypso and reggae styles. Punta rock unites Garifuna and Creole musical traditions. Some of the Garifuna musicians who developed this style are Andy Palacio, Pen Cayetano, and Mohobub Flores.

A Creole style that has lost ground to modern international music is the calypso-like breakdown. Breakdowns have much in common with Garifuna punta because they, too, use songs to criticize local personalities or relate humorous incidents.

In the 1940s steel bands performed in Belize City at Christmastime, and singers like William Trapp and Roderick Brown improvised breakdowns about that year's significant events or some notable British personality. These songs would then be popular all year long until the next round of breakdowns was crafted. Today's breakdowns may not compete with modern Top 40 tunes, but Christmas continues to be a season of spontaneous musical celebrations of singing and drumming called *brams*.

Breakdown evolved from the music and dance of loggers, especially a form called *buru*.

Belizean performers tuning their instruments.

Philip Lewis specializes in pen-and-ink drawings of Caye Caulker, where he makes his home. His drawings are simple and uncomplicated and capture snapshots of daily life.

The Garifuna and Creoles are renowned drummers, and they have developed Belizean forms of drums from local materials. Typical Garifuna drum performances involve three drums of various sizes that are made from cedar wood and turtle shells. Garifuna and Creole drumming can be heard during a spontaneous party or local festival. The concept of drums was imported with African slaves. Drums are central to African music and were used in Africa as a medium of communication between villages and as an essential element in religious performances. Slave owners tried to suppress drumming and dancing, but it survived despite their best efforts. Slaves would hold *gombays* (GOM-bays), or drumming and dancing parties, at which captives from different African tribes would compete in dancing and drumming. *Gombay* also refers to a type of Belizean drum made from goatskin and played with the hand.

Although not exclusively Belizean, the marimba is an integral part of the musical culture of Belize. This percussion instrument is often played by Mayans and mestizos during festivities and celebrations. It is a type of xylophone with a wooden resonator. The resonator is the part of the instrument that amplifies the sounds of the wooden crossbars being struck by mallets. Despite its popularity among the modern Maya, it is not a traditional Mayan instrument. The marimba came to the New World with African slaves but was later adopted by indigenous and mestizo people. Mestizo and Mayan musicians have also adopted instruments from the Spanish tradition such as guitars and violins.

CRAFTS

Most tourists want some artwork to take home as a reminder of their visit to Belize, and Belizean craftspeople are more than happy to comply. Some traditional crafts have been revived or sustained because of this, and many new ones have been developed.

Mayan weavers, using natural plant fibers, produce beautiful and useful objects such as bags, baskets, and hammocks. These items are still used by the people themselves, but sales to tourists bring in much needed cash to households and empowers the women who make them with some financial independence. Stone carving was a highly developed art form among the ancient Mayans, but modern Mayan people no longer build and carve beautiful stone temples as in the past. Today, however, carving has been revived for the tourist industry and for export. Popular materials include the nut of the cohune palm, coconut shell, and slate.

Ceramics are created all over the country, featuring motifs from nature and Mayan art. Musical instruments are also made for sale, particularly Garifuna and Creole drums. Creole and Garifuna women produce handmade dolls. Such dolls tend to be adult black women either dressed in their finest clothes or performing a domestic task. Mennonites craft wooden furniture that is simple, functional, beautiful, and much sought after by locals and tourists.

A Garifuna girl's homemade doll.

LEISURE

Local workers unwinding on
hammocks after a long day.

BELIZE IS, IN MANY WAYS, QUITE similar to developed countries in its leisure activities and pastimes, although the very idea of leisure is a newcomer in everyday Belizean life.

THE HISTORY OF LEISURE IN BELIZE

As a logging camp, Belize Town offered little in the way of entertainment. Loggers worked hard in the forests cutting timber and returned to town to sell their logs to merchant ships. When the ships arrived in port, they announced their arrival with a canon shot. The most popular trade item was rum, brought from other West Indian sugar colonies. The loggers would squander their earnings aboard these ships in drink and revelry. As the colony became more settled, an annual festival was held during Christmas. Merchants would set up stalls in Belize to sell rum and food, and the loggers would party with abandon for days on end. As the British gained more control in the early 19th century, the Christmas tradition changed. British commanders would muster all able-bodied men into the Citizen's Militia for the week leading up to Christmas. Businesses were shut as their owners did their annual military training. There were balls and amusements but not the wild carousing of past times. This practice lasted until the repeal of the Militia Law in 1846.

Protestant Wesleyan missionaries finally brought the unruly celebrations to an end, bidding instead for abstinence and sobriety. This damper lasted well into the 20th century. As late as 1945, the only social gatherings sanctioned by law were those related to the church. There were no separate theaters or nightlife in the form of dance clubs

The few movie theaters in Belize, mainly show films from the United States and India. Dish antennas now receive more than fifty television channels through satellite signals, and locals can watch international news, live sports, and Spanish-language telenovelas (soap operas) from Venezuela and Mexico.

109

or bars. Private parties were supervised by the police. Of course, this somber situation has changed dramatically. Today there are bars, clubs, and dance halls in larger towns, and people are no longer required to register their private parties. Fun has come a long way in Belize!

ENTERTAINMENT

Television came to Belize fairly recently. Before the days of television, the primary social activity was talking with neighbors and friends. Men, in particular, would meet in public places after the day's work to discuss life's vagaries. Every village has a café or local store that sells drinks where people can gather to chat. Women meet in other places, such as at church events, along the street, or at the market. In small towns and villages gossip is not only highly entertaining but also an integral part of social life. Gossip is a form of information exchange, keeping people abreast of developments among their neighbors. It also solidifies social groups by creating a group histories. People who gossip together affirm that they have a long-standing relationship. There were also organized church events. In addition to Sunday devotions, there would occasionally be dances or picnics.

A beach bar in Caye Caulker is a restaurant and more, with patrons playing the marimba.

Birth, marriage, and death also provided entertainment. It may seem odd to talk about celebrating death, but among Creoles and Garifuna, there is an element of enjoyment in a funeral, since everyone participates in it. At events such as weddings and funerals, storytelling and music are essential elements. Stories, legends, and folktales often contain bits of history and information about cultural values and beliefs. Listening to the stories of the elders is one way for children to learn about their culture and for adults to reaffirm their beliefs. Music and dance are indispensable parts of entertainment in Belize.

Belizeans catching the morning news.

RADIO AND TELEVISION

The first radio broadcasts heard around Belize City took place in 1937. Those who could afford it bought radios and always made allowance in the family budget for batteries. There was even a fad for country-and-western music in the 1940s because Belizean radio could pick up Texas stations. In 1952 Radio Belize opened its doors as the only legal national radio station.

Before telephones and television sets were available, the radio was everyone's main source of information about the world, the country, and each other, as Radio Belize used to devote a segment of its programs to delivering personal messages. In this way, Belizeans who were away from home could learn about a sick relative or other emergencies. Listening to the evening broadcast every day was a focal point of people's lives. Apart from news and weather, the radio also brought a variety of music styles to people listening in different parts of the country. Radio Belize regularly devoted up to a third of its airtime to Spanish-language broadcasts and music from Mexico and other Spanish-speaking countries in the region. Today, it is estimated that all Belizeans have access to a radio.

There was no Belizean television station before the 1970s as the population was too small to warrant one. In 1978 an American entrepreneur sent video movies to ten Belizeans for rental to others and started a craze for television sets and videocassette players. Enterprising Belizeans soon built receivers to pirate television signals from Mexico and the United States. Belizeans are crazy about TV, and cable TV is widely available in all towns and cities—including the suburbs. Cable television rates average $15 a month, and these generally include about 65 channels with all the goodies such as CNN, HBO, STARZ, Cinemax, Showtime, and of course ABC, CBS, NBC, and FOX. The local cable operators also throw in British, Mexican, Indian, Chinese, and pay-per-view channels for good measure. There is satellite TV as well, and being so close to North America, the satellite footprint of most television signals covers Belize with excellent picture quality.

Catching up with friends and family is a breeze for this tourist in an Internet café on the beach in Belize.

More than 24 radio stations exist in Belize today, half of which are religious broadcasters run by U.S. evangelical groups. The other half is commercial radio.

INTERNET

Electronic mail and Internet access became available in 1995 through the efforts of a Canadian student who was working as a volunteer. Belize had 60,000 Internet users as of March 2010, which was 19.1 percent of the population. Until recently, the telephone company in Belize was the only one allowed to offer Internet services. Along with satellite Internet, both Direct TV and Starband (satellite television channels) now offer satellite Internet access, and hundreds of Belizeans have jumped on the bandwagon. Belize, just like everywhere else on the globe, is totally accessible through the magic of the Internet.

SPORTS, GAMES, AND FADS

The most popular local team sport is soccer, called football in Belize. It became popular in England near the end of the 19th century and spread to Belize from there. Racing is also very popular. There are many regular bicycle races, sailing races, and horse races. Most Belizeans live near water and enjoy swimming as a pastime. Among the games favored by Belizeans are bingo and checkers. Gambling, both legal and illegal, is also popular. Legal gambling includes such institutions as the National Lottery or Boledo (boh-LAY-doh), and slot machines are turning up in tourist resorts. There are two casinos in the country, the biggest of which is Princess Hotel and Casino Belize, located in Belize City. A smaller Princess Casino is in San Ignacio, about 80 miles (130 km) from Belize City. Clubs and discos are frequented by young Belizeans who follow local, Caribbean, and North American music and dance fads. A noteworthy trend that has caught on is nature conservation and appreciation. Belizeans have become aware of the vast natural beauty around them and are working hard to preserve it.

Soccer is the most popular sport in Belize. This is followed closely by basketball, baseball, and softball. Horse-racing meets usually take place during festival periods and bicycle races are held frequently. Other well-loved sports include polo and boxing.

Basketball has become a very popular sport among teenagers.

FESTIVALS

Singers on Hopkins Beach celebrating the anniversary of the arrival of the Garifuna in Belize.

FOR SUCH A SMALL COUNTRY, Belize has many festivals and holidays. Some commemorate special days in Belizean national history, while others are celebrated by specific cultural or religious groups.

NATIONAL HOLIDAYS

National holidays do not have a religious basis such as Christmas or Easter. In Belize, as in many countries, Labor Day is celebrated on May 1. The minister of labor usually gives a public address at this time, and

Teenage girls wearing their marching band uniforms at a celebration in Belize.

Among the local Creoles, all national celebrations are accompanied by open-air dancing called jump-up. Almost all the villages, particularly those along the Caribbean coast, have their own discos playing speciality Afro-Caribbean music.

Bull riding is a favorite event at the National Agricultural Fair.

there are parades of workers and rallies around the country. There are also kite contests, bicycle races, regattas (sailing races), and horse races. Another national holiday is Independence Day on September 21. This is the formal date of independence from the British in 1981. Since Saint George's Caye Day on September 10 is also a holiday commemorating Belizean history and national pride, the whole month of September tends to become a time of celebration. Independence is marked with flag-raising ceremonies, parades, and street celebrations. Other national holidays include Garifuna Settlement Day and Columbus Day.

AGRICULTURAL FAIRS AND SPORTS EVENTS

There are a number of fairs held each year to mark Belize's progress in agriculture. The annual Agriculture and Trade Show is held in Belmopan each spring and now attracts more than 50,000 visitors. Livestock and produce are exhibited, and there are dance performances, a rodeo, and displays of local handicrafts. Companies from Mexico, Guatemala, Honduras, and El Salvador participate in the trade show as well.

Local sports are also featured throughout the year beginning with the International Billfish Tournament in February. The Belize Game Fish Association sponsors this competition among fishermen to land a marlin weighing more than 500 pounds (227 kg). Prize money of some $50,000 is awarded! Commonwealth Day on May 24 is also marked by sports events. This day is celebrated in many former British colonies as the Queen's birthday. There are horse races in Belize City and Orange Walk, and cycle races between Cayo and Belmopan. Columbus Day celebrates indigenous cultures in the New World with sailing races in the harbor.

LOCAL FAIRS

While some celebrations are nationwide, others that reflect local pride and customs are confined to particular villages and towns. In the Maya community of San José Succotz, the day of the patron saint—San José, or Saint Joseph—is celebrated in April. There is plenty of entertainment, including rides, food, and live marimba music. San Ignacio celebrates its food and crafts in the Cayo Expo every May. Also in May is the Coconut Festival on Caye Caulker. Local residents design and build floats to compete in a parade. They dance and enjoy a community party with great food and drink.

A coconut toss competition under way during the Coconut Festival.

The Toledo Festival of Arts is a weeklong celebration in May when schoolchildren create plays that highlight the region's cultural diversity. Arts and crafts such as baskets, paintings, and clay sculptures are exhibited. In June San Pedro celebrates its patron saint and that of fishermen, Saint Peter. This is a three-day event. Part of the festivities includes a boat parade, the blessing of boats and fishermen, and a special Catholic mass. The mestizos of Orange Walk and Corozal participate in Mexico's National Day in September. Some townspeople even cross over into Mexico to visit with family and friends across the border.

CARNAVAL

As in many other Latin American countries where there are Roman Catholics, Carnaval (Spanish for "carnival," similar to Mardi Gras) is celebrated among Spanish speakers on Ambergris Caye. Carnaval is observed sometime in February or March, a few days before the beginning of Lent. Lent is a period of abstinence for Catholics, when many give up eating meat and other favorite foods and beverages. Since Lent is supposed to be a somber time of reflection on the crucifixion of Christ at Easter, the traditional European custom was to have a wild party beforehand. In San Pedro Carnaval is celebrated with games in which people throw flour and talcum powder on one another, and paint each other with lipstick or paint.

BARON BLISS DAY

Henry Edward Ernest Victor Bliss was the fourth Baron Bliss of the former Kingdom of Portugal. He was born and raised in England and first came to Belize in 1926 on his yacht, the *Sea King*. Due to illness, he never left the ship but spent several months anchored in the harbor, enjoying the climate and hospitality of Belize. He died in Belize and was buried there. He was so grateful for the kindness and respect shown to him by Belizeans that he left nearly $2 million as a trust fund for Belize. This money has been used to build clinics, water systems, and libraries. A portion of the fund is also used to host a yacht regatta every March 9, when Belize honors the baron's contributions. In addition to boat races, there are also horse and bicycle races around the country.

The Baron Bliss lighthouse and tomb in Belize City.

EASTER

As Belize is largely Christian, there is an official four-day national holiday at Easter. Celebrations differ among different Christian denominations. For example, on Ambergris Caye and Caye Caulker where most of the inhabitants are Roman Catholic, there are special church services on Good Friday and processions carrying the cross through the towns. On Holy Saturday the Cross Country Cycling Classic is held between Belize City and San Ignacio. Cyclists from Belize and abroad participate in this popular race along the Western Highway as far as San Ignacio and back to the grand finale in Belize City. Easter Sunday and Monday are marked by family get-togethers, sumptious food, meals, and church ceremonies.

The Cashew Festival at Crooked Tree celebrates this important cash crop.

THE CASHEW FESTIVAL

The Cashew Festival is held in Crooked Tree in northern Belize District on the first weekend of May to celebrate the cashew harvest. Cashew trees are native to this area, and their nuts are sold both raw and roasted. This festival is enlivened with storytelling, arts, crafts, music, dancing, feasts, folkloric performances, and Caribbean-style food, with an emphasis on cashew creations such as cashew jellies and wine. There are also demonstrations of cashew harvesting. This festival was actually created by a tour company based in the United States but has become a celebration of Belizean culture and the preservation of the natural environment.

NATIONAL DAY

Belize's National Day celebrates the Battle of Saint George's Caye, which took place in 1798 in the waters around Saint George's Caye near Belize City. It began on September 3 when 31 Spanish ships carrying 2,000 soldiers and 500 sailors converged at the mouth of the Belize River to attack the combined British and Baymen force, which was only 350 defenders! There was a British warship, the *Merlin*, with 50 men, and five local boats, *Towser, Tickler, Mermaid, Swinger,* and *Teaser*, each with 25 Baymen volunteers, and a number of small craft and rafts.

For the first few days, the Spanish tried to maneuver their ships so they could land their troops and establish a base on Saint George's Caye. Since the Baymen and the British knew the local waters much better than the attacking Spanish and had smaller and more manageable boats, they could position themselves to block the Spanish at every turn. Finally, the Spanish sent 14 rafts full of soldiers from their ships. Despite being greatly outnumbered, the British and Baymen valiantly fought off the attack. While the Spanish galleons were sitting immobile offshore, the British warship began to bombard them mercilessly. This attack lasted two and a half hours before the Spaniards decided to raise anchor and withdraw, leaving many dead Spaniards from this failed attack. Miraculously, not even one Bayman or British soldier was killed.

Patriotic marchers drum the way at the National Day celebrations in the capital.

The battle did not change the status of Belize, which at that time was not yet a formal British possession, but it was a source of local pride for the Baymen, and it has continued to represent Belize's national spirit of being small but being strong. This spirit is honored around the country during the days leading up to National Day, September 10, with parades, official ceremonies, pop music concerts, sporting activities, and a special parade of fire engines.

GARIFUNA SETTLEMENT DAY

The first large group of Garifuna arrived in Belize on November 19, 1832, led by Alejo Beni, the principal leader who helped them flee Honduras's civil war, and settled in Stann Creek. A few Garifuna lived there before then, but their presence was not significant. Nowadays, the week leading up to this day is busy with street dancing, drumming, and parties. Garifuna from all over the Caribbean region come to Belize for this important celebration of their culture. The festivities include a reenactment of the landing of Alejo Beni. There is also a religious ceremony, performed in the Garifuna language in

A reenactment of the 1832 landing of Alejo Beni, starting the pivotal Garifuna presence in Belize.

January 1	New Year's Day
March 9	Baron Bliss Day
March/April	Good Friday/Holy Saturday/Easter Sunday/Easter Monday
May 1	Labor Day
May 24	Commonwealth Day
September 10	National Day, also called Saint George's Caye Day
September 21	Independence Day
October 12	Columbus Day
November 19	Garifuna Settlement Day
December 25	Christmas Day

the Catholic church, that combines elements of Catholicism with African and Carib rituals. On that day, the main road in Dangriga is closed to traffic.

CARIBBEAN CHRISTMAS

In the weeks leading up to Christmas, Garifuna perform the John Canoe dance, also known as the Wanaragua, on the streets of Punta Gorda, Dangriga, and Belize City. This is a dance with specific roles for the male dancers. There is a "king," a "clown," and several boys costumed as pregnant women. Drummers and female singers accompany the dancers, who wear masks with mustaches, costumes, and decorative headdresses in lighthearted mimicry of the finery of the colonial European masters. The dancers move from house to house in Dangriga, Belize City, and other Garifuna settlements, performing for gifts of candy, rum, and money. The main dancer, the king, mimics the arrogant walk of a European slave owner, making people laugh. The John Canoe dance used to be performed in other parts of the Afro-Caribbean area such as Jamaica, but it seems to be dying out nowadays. It has become pure entertainment in Belize, although retaining elements that resemble ritualized rebellion against colonial authority.

FOOD

Fresh fish sold at a local market in Belize City.

BELIZE IS A PARADOX WHEN IT comes to food. There is a grand choice of foods available from land and sea, but most Belizeans are satisfied to eat a fairly monotonous diet. As also with lifestyle, there is no single standard— different ethnic groups and regions tend to favor different kinds of food.

The main meal in Belize is eaten at midday. For the mestizos, common staples include corn tortillas and beans, while the inner country residents enjoy more exotic fare, such as wild game, roast armadillo, and roast paca (a type of large rodent).

Children helping choose vegetables at a San Ignacio market.

Colorful food stands dot the sidewalks in Belize City.

BASIC FOOD

For most Belizeans, meals are usually accompanied by, or consist entirely of, beans and rice. Red or black beans are usually cooked in large batches with some sort of salted meat such as bacon for flavoring. Rice is the staple starch in the diet and is generally boiled. On special occasions rice will be cooked with coconut milk for added flavor and richness. Mayan people, particularly in the south, substitute corn for rice as their staple. They grow the corn themselves and use cornmeal to make the soft tortillas that are eaten with most meals. Nearer the coast, people eat more seafood, while those living inland depend more on chicken for protein. The Garifuna eat fish regularly and, on special occasions, will cook it in coconut milk for flavor. Coconut milk, made from squeezing the milk from grated coconut meat, is a standard ingredient in Caribbean cooking. A typical Creole Sunday meal is coconut rice, beans, and chicken with gravy.

Bread, either leavened or unleavened "quick" bread, is also part of the regular Belizean diet. Some quick breads are made from wheat flour, others from corn. For example, the southern Mayans grow corn and use the ground meal to make soft flat tortillas for everyday meals. On special occasions the Mayans will make tamales that are made with cornmeal, meat, and vegetables wrapped together in a banana leaf and then boiled. Another quick bread, called *bammie* or *bammy* (bah-mee), is made with cassava.

Making cassava bread is a two-day process. The cassava tubers have to be dug up, then peeled and grated into a pulp. Using a long tube strainer, the liquid is forced out of the pulp, dropping the pulp in clumps into a pan. These chunks are dried and grated into flour, which is spead over an iron griddle. The flour is pressed together and then baked over a fire to make the crisp cassava bread. Breadfruit and bananas can also be dried and ground into flour for making bread. Leavened breads are made with wheat flour and require yeast to make them rise. In the United States johnnycakes are made with cornmeal, but in Belize wheat flour is used to make johnnycakes, jacks, cakes, and fritters. Johnnycakes are a type of sweet pancake, while jacks are a puff pastry. Both are eaten for breakfast with fruit preserves.

VARIETY

Although Belizeans have a fairly monotonous diet, it is also true that there are foods and methods of preparation available that are fantastic in their variety. The forests contain all sorts of wild game available to hunters. For example, the gibnut or paca, a rabbitlike rodent, was served to Queen Elizabeth II on her formal visit some years ago. There are wild ducks, iguanas and iguana eggs, deer, armadillo, and peccary. The southern Mayans cook wild game in spicy sauces.

The sea and rivers provide their own vast bounty. Conch, shark, sea turtle, lobster, squid, red snapper, shrimp, sea bass, and barracuda can be found along the coast and by the cays. Although sea turtles are an endangered species, Belizean law allows hunting them at certain times of the year. Conch is one of nature's most versatile foods and is delicious. For seafood lovers who cannot decide which fish or shellfish they prefer, there is "boil up." This is a stew made from whatever could be caught that day, cooked with coconut milk and spices. Sweet potatoes, tomatoes, peppers, squash, pumpkin, and avocados are all native to Central America. Mangoes, guava, pawpaws, bananas, plantain, grapefruit, and breadfruit also grow there.

Tortillas made in home kitchens, as shown by this girl in Laguna Village, are staples in every district.

Marie Sharp's popular fiery hot habanero sauce.

SEASONING

Belizeans know how to use spices and herbs to add just the right flavor to any dish. Their repertoire of seasonings is drawn from diverse traditions and cuisines. Among the more familiar seasonings are basil, bay leaf, cilantro, dill, garlic, ginger, marjoram, mint, oregano, sage, thyme, and parsley. Others are more exotic, such as achiote or annatto (a fruit boiled to form a paste used in cooking). East Indians have introduced curry to Belize. Mayan and Mexican traditions have contributed two other mixed seasonings in the form of pastes: red recardo and black recardo. The red version uses annatto, garlic, black pepper, onion, and vinegar that is packed into balls and is used in tamales and meat dishes. Black recardo combines burned corn tortillas, onion, garlic, cloves, black pepper, and vinegar and is used with bean fillings. The Garifuna use seaweed to flavor certain dishes.

Belizeans use a variety of hot peppers to add zing to their food. The most common is the habanero pepper. Belize is home to a famous hot sauce—Marie Sharp's. Marie Sharp's Fine Foods Ltd. began its operation in 1982 and is a small, family-run business in the foothills of the Maya Mountains in the district of Stann Creek. The company buys fruit and vegetables from local growers, which supports small-scale agriculture in the region. Besides its famous hot sauce, it also produces jam, spreads, and other sauces. The hot sauce contains habanero peppers, carrots, onions, lime juice, vinegar, garlic, and spices. It is found on most Belizean tables and can now be bought in the United States.

Belizean beans and rice is different from the standard rice and beans. The Belizean version is a national dish that Belizeans take pride in serving. The beans are cooked together with the rice. With standard rice and beans, the beans are cooked separately, then spooned over the rice.

In 2002 a survey done in Belize on food safety found that a large segment of the population had alarming food safety practices (or food unsafety practices). Sixty-three percent of respondents to the survey said that they did not refrigerate poultry, meat, or fish within two hours of cooking. One-third thought unrefrigerated fish was safe to eat, 15.8 percent had domestic animals entering the kitchen, one-third had rats and mice entering the kitchen, 29 percent saw cockroaches and flies in the kitchen, one-third had uncovered garbage storage areas outside the kitchen, and 13.6 percent had uncovered garbage areas inside the kitchen.

With such astonishing data, the Ministry of Health ran a Food Safety Awareness Campaign in 2005 to correct the negligent food handling practices of the Belizean public. It was active for eight weeks and included videos, pamphlets, stickers, brochures, and newspaper and radio advertisements. The results were very positive, and the overall number of food poisoning cases in Belize went down. The campaign was well received by the Belizean public, who appreciated the efforts to inform them about safe food handling. The National Consultation on Promoting Food Safety among Consumers in Belize met in 2010 to discuss how they can better promote food safety in the country.

BEVERAGES

As in many tropical countries, the most refreshing Belizean drinks are made with fresh fruit. Almost any fruit can be combined with water or ice to make a delicious drink. Belize also produces its own soft drinks that are widely available, in addition to well-known foreign brands. Belikin beer is the local brand, and Belizeans are quite proud of it. Rum is produced from sugarcane. The Garifuna have a couple of alternative alcoholic drinks such as cashew wine and "local dynamite," a combination of rum and coconut milk. For a nonalcoholic energy drink, there is chicory-flavored coffee. Mint is brewed in hot water to make a refreshing tea.

The local Belikin beer is served at most meals.

BELIZEAN BEANS AND RICE

4 servings

1 cup (225 g) dried red beans

1 teaspoon (5 ml) dried thyme

3 tablespoons (45 ml) yellow onion, chopped

1 clove garlic, finely chopped

1½ teaspoons (7½ ml) black pepper

1 tablespoon (15 g) salt

½ cup (120 ml) coconut milk

2 cups (450 g) white rice

Wash the beans. Add new water to cover the beans. Soak for 4—8 hours or overnight. Discard the water and rinse the beans in cold water. Place beans in a pot and add the garlic and onion. Add about 4 cups of water. Bring to a boil, then lower heat, cover, and simmer the beans until tender, for about one and a half hours. A pressure cooker may be used to cut down the time. Season the beans with black pepper, thyme, and salt. Add coconut milk and stir. Bring to a boil. Add the raw rice to the seasoned beans. Stir  and then cover. Cook on low heat until the water is absorbed and rice is tender, about 25 to 30 minutes. If necessary, add more water gradually until rice is done.

Note: Usually, one cup of rice absorbs two cups of water, although rice grains can vary in the amount of water they absorb. To warm up any leftover beans and rice, sprinkle the dish with water to moisten it, cover, and heat for a short time in a microwave oven.

PONE (SWEET POTATO POUND)

16 servings

2 pounds (1 kg) sweet potatoes

2 cups (450 g) brown sugar

2 teaspoons (10 ml) vanilla extract

1 teaspoon (5 ml) nutmeg

1 cup (225 g) raisins

2—4 ounces (55—110 g) fresh ginger, grated

4 cups (1 L) milk (evaporated or coconut)

2 tablespoons (30 g) margarine (melted)

Grease a 9" by 13" baking pan or Pyrex dish. Preheat oven to 450°F (230°C). Wash, peel, and grate the sweet potatoes. In a large bowl, add the grated sweet potatoes, sugar, vanilla extract, nutmeg, raisins, and ginger. Mix well. Add the milk and margarine. Mix well. Put in baking pan or Pyrex dish. Place on bottom shelf of oven for 35—40 minutes. Then move dish to top shelf and lower oven temperature to 350°F (180°C). Bake for about 60—80 minutes more until brown. Check by inserting a toothpick into the center, which should come out clean. The top should have a jellied, sticky look.

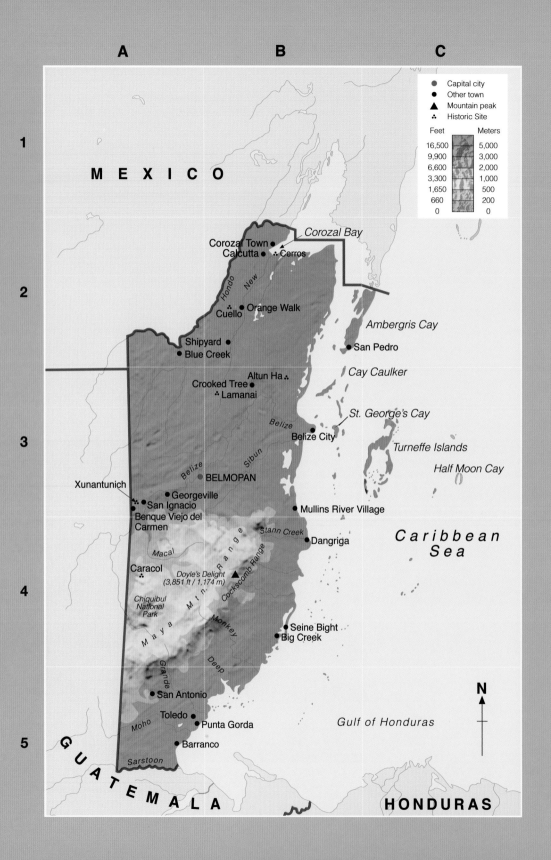

A   **B**   **C**

1

M E X I C O

Capital city
Other town
Mountain peak
Historic Site

Feet	Meters
16,500	5,000
9,900	3,000
6,600	2,000
3,300	1,000
1,650	500
660	200
0	0

Corozal Town •
Corozal Bay
Calcutta • • Cerros

2

Hondo
New

Cuello ⚬ • Orange Walk

Shipyard •
Blue Creek •

Ambergris Cay

• San Pedro

Altun Ha ⚬
Crooked Tree •
⚬ Lamanai

Cay Caulker

Belize

Sibun

St. George's Cay

Belize City •

Turneffe Islands

3

Belize

BELMOPAN

Half Moon Cay

Xunantunich ⚬
• Georgeville
⚬ San Ignacio
Benque Viejo del
Carmen

• Mullins River Village

*C a r i b b e a n
S e a*

Macal

Stann Creek
Range

Dangriga •

Caracol ⚬
Doyle's Delight ▲
(3,851 ft / 1,174 m)

Cockscomb Range

4

Chiquibul
National
Park

M
a
y
a

Monkey

Mtn.
Range

Seine Bight •
Big Creek •

Grande

Deep

San Antonio •

N

Toledo •
• Punta Gorda

Gulf of Honduras

5

Moho

• Barranco

G
Sarstoon

U
A
T
E
M
A
L
A

HONDURAS

MAP OF BELIZE

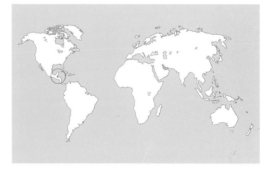

ECONOMIC BELIZE

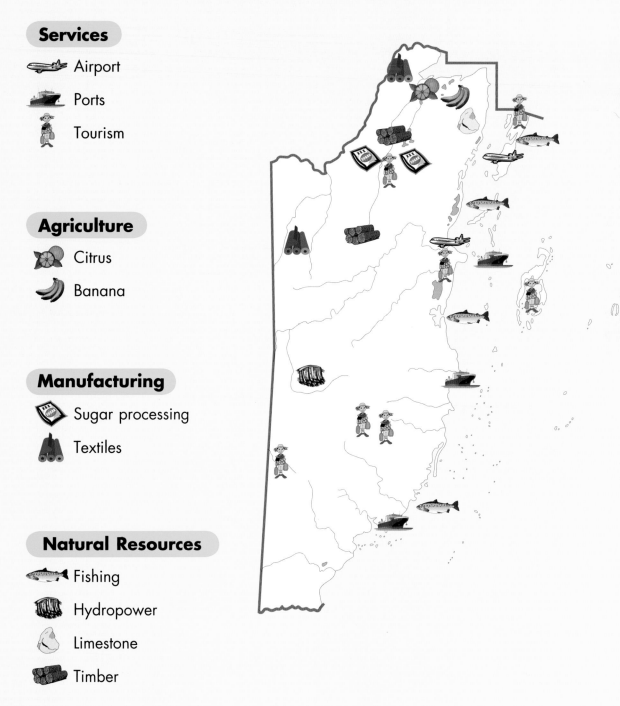

Services
- ✈ Airport
- 🚢 Ports
- 🧑 Tourism

Agriculture
- 🍊 Citrus
- 🍌 Banana

Manufacturing
- 🏭 Sugar processing
- Textiles

Natural Resources
- 🐟 Fishing
- Hydropower
- Limestone
- Timber

ABOUT THE ECONOMY

OVERVIEW

In this small, essentially private-enterprise economy, tourism is the number one foreign exchange earner, followed by exports of marine products, citrus fruits, cane sugar, bananas, and clothing. The government's expansionary policies, initiated in September 1998, led to sturdy GDP growth averaging nearly 4 percent in the 1999—2007 period, though growth slipped to 2.1 percent in 2008 and to -1.5 percent in 2009 as a result of the global slowdown, natural disasters, and a drop in the price of oil. Oil discoveries in 2006 bolstered economic growth somewhat. Exploration efforts continue and production increased a small amount in 2009. Major concerns continue to be the sizable trade deficit and foreign debt. In February 2007 the government restructured nearly all of its public external commercial debt, which helped to reduce interest payments and to relieve some of the country's liquidity concerns. A key short-term objective remains the reduction of poverty with the help of international donors.

GROSS DOMESTIC PRODUCT (GDP)

$2.485 billion (2009 estimate)

CURRENCY

Belize dollars
1 US$ = BZD $1.96 (2010 estimate)

GDP GROWTH

-1.5 percent (2009 estimate)

LAND USE

Arable land: 3.05 percent, permanent crops: 1.39 percent, other: 95.56 percent

NATURAL RESOURCES

Arable land potential, hydropower, timber, fish

AGRICULTURAL PRODUCTS

Bananas, cacao, citrus fruits, sugarcane, fish, shrimp, lumber

MAJOR EXPORTS

Sugar, bananas, citrus fruits, clothing, fish products, molasses, wood, crude oil

MAJOR IMPORTS

Machinery and transportation equipment, manufactured goods, fuels, chemicals, pharmaceuticals, food, beverages, tobacco

MAIN TRADE PARTNERS

United States, United Kingdom, Mexico, Cuba, Guatemala, Italy, Côte d'Ivoire, Nigeria

WORKFORCE

122,300 (2008 estimate)

UNEMPLOYMENT RATE

8.1 percent (2008 estimate)

INFLATION

0.3 percent (2009 estimate)

EXTERNAL DEBT

$954.1 million (2008 estimate)

CULTURAL BELIZE

Ambergris Caye
The largest of the cays that dot the coast of Belize, the coastline of Ambergris Caye is protected by the Barrier Reef, and the island supports all water sports. Several nearby snorkeling and scuba sites offer excellent opportunities for viewing coral and marine life.

Hol Chan Marine Reserve
Belize's most popular snorkeling and diving site, this park encompasses 5 square miles (13 square km) of protected area made up of coral formations, sea grass beds, and mangroves.

Lamanai Archaeological Site
Lamanai is one of Belize's largest Mayan ceremonial centers. The ruins are located on the banks of the New River and are set in secondary tropical forest. The site also includes the ruins of two Christian churches and a sugar mill.

Caye Caulker
On Caye Caulker there are no cars, no fumes, and no hassles; there are just white sandy beaches, balmy breezes, azure waters, fresh seafood, and a fantastic barrier reef at its doorstep. The island is an ideal base for snorkeling and diving adventures at the nearby reef.

Altun Ha Archaeological Site
Altun Ha is northern Belize's most famous Mayan ruin. The community existed from 600 B.C. until the collapse of the Classic Mayan civilization in A.D. 900. It is famous for the discovery of the Jade Head, the largest carved jade object found in the entire Mayan area.

Barton Creek Caves
Visitors to the Barton Creek cave system enter it by canoe. Inside, observers can see ancient Mayan skeletal remains and unbelievably giant stalactites and stalagmites. These caves represented the Mayan realm of Xibalba, which the Mayan believed was a link of sorts to the spiritual world.

Belize Barrier Reef
The reef is second in size only to the Great Barrier Reef in Australia. It is some 185 miles (298 km) long, and never exceeds 25 miles (40 km) offshore of Belize in any spot. The reef is both impressive and fairly easy to access, ideal for diving and snorkeling among a wide variety of marine animals.

Actun Tunichil Muknal Cave
Visitors hike to the wide cave opening and start their tour of the cave by swimming across a deep pool. Once inside, participants hike and climb through the cave surrounded by giant flowstone rock formations, which drip from the ceiling and grow up from the cave floor. Caverns contain Mayan sacrificed human skeletons and other offerings.

Blue Hole Natural Monument
Located in the center of the Lighthouse Reef Atoll, the monument is a circular limestone sinkhole of vivid blue water measuring 412 feet (126 m) deep and 1,000 feet (305 m) across. The Great Blue Hole offers divers interesting observations of distinctive, bizarre limestone stalactites attached to its walls and a variety of fish species.

El Caracol
Once a great Mayan city-state, El Caracol is now one of the country's largest archaeological sites; it claims the tallest manmade structure in the land. El Caracol is cradled in the foothills of Belize's Maya Mountains at an elevation of around 1,500 feet (457 meters).

Dangriga
Dangriga is the largest town in southern Belize, and the spiritual capital of the country's Garifuna people. It is the birthplace of punta rock and is home to a number of notable Garifuna artists, artisans, and festivals, not to mention Belize's only Garifuna museum.

ABOUT THE CULTURE

OFFICIAL NAME
Belize

TOTAL AREA
8,867 square miles (22,966 square km)

CAPITAL
Belmopan

LAND AREA
8,805 square miles (22,806 square km)

POPULATION
314,522 (2010 estimate)

MAJOR TOWNS
Belize City, Belmopan, Orange Walk, San Ignacio, Corozal Town, Dangriga

HIGHEST POINT
Doyle's Delight (3,851 feet or 1,174 m)

MAJOR RIVERS
Belize, New, Hondo, Sibun, Monkey, Deep, Rio Grande, Moho, Sarstoon

CAYS
Ambergris, Caulker, Saint George's, Half Moon, Turneffe Islands

ETHNIC GROUPS
Mestizo 48.7 percent, Creole 24.9 percent, Maya 10.6 percent, Garifuna 6.1 percent, other 9.7 percent

RELIGION
Roman Catholic 49.6 percent, Protestant 27 percent (Pentecostal 7.4 percent, Anglican 5.3 percent, Seventh-day Adventist 5.2 percent, Mennonite 4.1 percent, Methodist 3.5 percent, Jehovah's Witnesses 1.5 percent), others 14 percent, none 9.4 percent

BIRTHRATE
27.3 births per 1,000 Belizeans (2009 estimate)

DEATH RATE
5.8 deaths per 1,000 Belizeans (2009 estimate)

AGE STRUCTURE
0—14 years: 37.9 percent
15—64 years: 58.6 percent
65 years and over: 3.5 percent (2009 estimate)

NATIONAL PLANT AND ANIMAL
Mahogany tree and Baird's tapir

MAIN LANGUAGES
Spanish 46 percent, Creole 32.9 percent, Mayan dialects 8.9 percent, English 3.9 percent (official), Garifuna 3.4 percent, German 3.3 percent, others 1.6 percent

LITERACY
People aged 15 years and older who can both read and write: 76.9 percent (2000 estimate)

TIME LINE

IN BELIZE	IN THE WORLD
1500–1000 B.C. Earliest evidence for actual Mayan settlements at Cuello, Santa Rita, and Colha in northern Belize.	**753 B.C.** Rome is founded.
A.D. 100–700 Construction of large temple pyramids at Lamanai and Cerros. Mayan civilization fully established throughout region.	**A.D. 600** Height of the Mayan civilization.
701–1200 Decline of many Maya cities in northern Belize, while Lamanai and Santa Rita still thrive.	**1000** The Chinese perfect gunpowder and begin to use it in warfare.
1200–1400 Increasing relations between Maya cities in Belize and northern Yucatán powers. Murals at Santa Rita (Corozal) created.	**1206–1368** Genghis Khan unifies the Mongols and starts conquest of the world. At its height, the Mongol Empire under Kublai Khan stretches from China to Persia and parts of Europe and Russia.
1502 First contact between Spanish and Mayans in the Bay of Honduras.	
1511–1519 Shipwrecked Spaniards land on coast of Yucatán. Spaniard Gonzalo Guerrero marries daughter of Nachan Can, ruler of ancient Chetumal.	**1530** Beginning of transatlantic slave trade organized in Africa by the Portuguese.
1600s The area of present-day Belize becomes part of Spain's possessions in Central America and the Caribbean; British buccaneers and woodcutters begin to settle around the Belize River.	**1558–1603** Reign of Elizabeth I of England.
1763–1783 Spain signs treaties granting British subjects the privilege of woodcutting but retains sovereignty.	**1776** U.S. Declaration of Independence
1862 Belize formally declared a British crown colony and named British Honduras.	**1789–1799** The French Revolution
1893 Mexico renounces claim to Belizean territory.	**1869** The Suez Canal is opened.
1981 Belize becomes independent with George Price as prime minister, but Guatemala refuses to recognize it.	**1914** World War I begins.
	1986 Nuclear power disaster at Chernobyl in Ukraine.
1991 Guatemala recognizes Belize as a sovereign and independent state.	**1991** Breakup of the Soviet Union.

IN BELIZE	IN THE WORLD

1998
Said Musa becomes the prime minister after the PUP wins a landslide election victory.

2001
Towns flattened, thousands left homeless after Hurricane Iris hits.

2001
Terrorists crash planes into New York, Washington D.C., and Pennsylvania.

2002
Belize and Guatemala agree on a draft settlement to their border dispute at talks brokered by the Organization of American States (OAS).

2003
Said Musa is elected for a second term as prime minister.

2003
War in Iraq begins.

2004
Britain's Privy Council dismisses an appeal to overturn the Belize government's approval of the proposed Chalillo Dam. Opponents say the dam threatens rare species and communities downstream.

2005
Public and private sector workers strike over budget measures, including tax and salary increases. Rioting breaks out in the capital during a wave of antigovernment protests.

2006
Belize begins commercial exploitation of its oil reserves.

2007
Organization of American States (OAS) recommends that border dispute with Guatemala be referred to International Court of Justice (ICJ).

2008
Dean Barrow becomes prime minister after the United Democratic Party (UDP) wins a landslide election victory.

2008
Barack Obama, the first black president of the United States, is elected.

2009
In Belize a magnitude 7.1 earthquake collapses more than 2 dozen homes, killing at least 6 people. Prime Minister Dean Barrow rushes through the nationalization of Belize Telemedia, the country's dominant telecommunications company, and appoints a new board of directors.

GLOSSARY

bammie (bah-mee)
A type of bread made with cassava starch, also spelled bammy.

Boledo (boh-LAY-doh)
The national lottery of Belize.

bram
A spontaneous musical celebration of singing and drumming.

breakdown
A type of music performed at Christmas with calypso bands in which the words parody and make fun of local figures.

Carnaval (CAR-na-val)
A festival just before Lent. Called Carnival or Mardi Gras elsewhere.

cenote (suh-NOH-tee)
A deep natural well or sinkhole, especially in Central America, formed by the collapse of surface limestone that exposes groundwater underneath.

chicle
A gumlike substance obtained from the latex of a tropical American tree, such as the sapodilla, used in the making of chewing gum.

duendes (doo-EN-days)
Mythical dwarfs who live in forests, evil but possess magical powers.

dugu (DOO-goo)
A Garifuna ancestral rite, meaning Feasting of the Dead, held to appease the spirit of a deceased ancestor.

escabeche (ES-kah-BAY-chay)
Also known as seviche, this dish is prepared by marinating raw seafood in lime or lemon juice.

gombay (GOM-bay)
Drumming and dancing party held by African slaves. Also a drum made of goatskin.

hickatee (hik-ah-TEE)
Central American river turtle.

johnnycake
A flat cake or bread made with a wheat flour batter in Belize, usually cooked on a griddle, like a pancake.

karst (kahrst)
An area of limestone terrain characterized by sinks, ravines, and underground streams.

marimba
A wooden percussion musical instrument—a type of xylophone—brought to the New World by African slaves, became popular among the Mayans.

mauger (MAH-ger)
A season of no wind in August.

monoculture
The use of land for growing only one type of crop.

Rastafarianism
A religious sect that regards the late Haile Selassie I of Ethiopia as the Messiah and Africa as the promised land, prominently followed by black Jamaicans.

FOR FURTHER INFORMATION

BOOKS

Berman, Joshua. *Moon Belize* (Moon Handbooks). Berkeley, CA: Avalon Travel Publishing, 2009.

Curling, Debbie. *Pancho's Great Adventures* (BELIZE). Bloomington, IN: Xlibris Corporation, 2009.

Lutz, Dick. *Belize: Reefs, Rain Forests, and Mayan Ruins.* Salem, OR: DIMI Press, 2005.

Miller, Debra A. *Belize* (Modern Nations of the World). Farmington Hills, MI: Lucent Books, 2003.

Schurch, Maylan. *Danger Signals in Belize* (Justin Case Adventures). Hagerstown, MD: Review & Herald Publishing, 2002.

Shields, Charles J. *Belize* (Central America Today). Broomall, PA: Mason Crest Publishers, 2008.

Sluder, Lan. *Fodor's Belize (with El Petén).* New York: Fodor's Travel Publications, 2010.

Streissguth, Thomas. *Belize in Pictures* (Visual Geography, Second Series). Minneapolis, MN: Twenty-First Century Books, 2009.

Vorhees, Mara and Joshua Samuel Brown. *Belize* (Country Guide). Oakland, CA: Lonely Planet, 2008.

WEBSITES

Belize Government's Official Portal, The. www.belize.gov.bz/

Belize Net. www.belize.net/search/npl.cgi

Belize Tourism Board. www.travelbelize.org/

CIA World Factbook Belize. https://www.cia.gov/library/publications/the-world-factbook/index.html

FILMS

Dive Travel: Belize, Home of the Famous Blue Hole. www.TravelVideoStore.com, under North America category, February 2009.

Equitrekking Season Three-Belize. www.TravelVideoStore.com, January 2010.

MUSIC

Various Artists. *Traditional Music of the Garifuna of Belize.* Smithsonian Folkways, 2009.

Various Artists. *Garifuna Music: Field Recordings from Belize.* Arc Music, 2005.

Various Artists. *Cult Cargo: Belize City Boil Up.* Numero, 2005.

BIBLIOGRAPHY

BOOKS

Barry, T. *Inside Belize.* Albuquerque, NM: The Interhemispheric Resource Center, 1995.

Berman, Joshua. *Moon Belize* (Moon Handbooks). Berkeley, CA: Avalon Travel Publishing, 2009.

Bolland, O. N. *Belize: A New Nation in Central America.* Boulder, CO: Westview Press, 1986.

Eltringham, Peter. *The Rough Guide to Belize 4* (Rough Guide Travel Guides). New York: Rough Guides; 4th edition, 2007.

Greenspan, Eliot. *Frommer's Belize* (Frommer's Complete). Hoboken, NJ: John Wiley & Sons, 3rd edition, 2008.

Lutz, Dick. *Belize: Reefs, Rain Forests, and Mayan Ruins.* Salem, OR: DIMI Press, 2005.

Mahler, R. *Belize: Adventures in Nature.* Santa Fe, NM: John Muir Publications, 1999.

Olson, J. S. *Indians of Central and South America.* Westport, CT: Greenwood Press, 1991.

Rabinowitz, Alan. *Jaguar: One Man's Struggle to Establish the World's First Jaguar Preserve.* Island Press Shearwater Books. Washington, D.C., 2000.

Sluder, Lan. *Fodor's Belize (with El Petén).* New York: Fodor's, 2010.

Sutherland, A. *The Making of Belize: Globalization in the Margins.* Westport, CT: Bergin & Garvey, 1998.

Tenenbaum, B. A., Ed. *Encyclopedia of Latin American History and Culture.* New York: Simon & Schuster Macmillan, 1996.

Vorhees, Mara and Joshua Samuel Brown. *Belize* (Country Guide). Oakland, CA: Lonely Planet, 2008.

Matola, Sharon and Sutherland, Allan. *The Further Adventures of Hoodwink the Owl.* Conservation International, 1993.

WEBSITES

Belize: A Virtual Guide. www.belizeexplorer.com/

Belize Chamber of Commerce and Industry, The. www.belize.org/bcci/

Belize Government's Official Portal, The. www.belize.gov.bz/

Belize National Parks and Wildlife Sanctuaries. http://centralamerica.com/belize/parks/index.htm

Belize Net: Search Engine of Information on Belize. www.belize.net/search/npl.cgi

Belize Tourism Board. www.travelbelize.org/

Belize Travel Information and Country Guide. www.belize.com/

CIA World Fact Book—Belize. https://www.cia.gov/library/publications/the-world-factbook/index.html

GoTo—Belize. www.goto-belize.com/index.htm

TouristClick: Belize National Parks Guide and Directory. www.touristclick.com/CentralAmerica_Belize_NationalParks.html

Travel Belize. www.travelbelize.org/german/html/guide/pa/pahp.html

INDEX

INDEX